KOREANS
TO REMEMBER

KOREANS
TO REMEMBER
Fifty Famous People Who
Helped Shape Korea

by
Richard Saccone

HOLLYM

Copyright © 1993
by Richard Saccone

All rights reserved

First published in 1993
Second printing, December 1993
by Hollym International Corp.
18 Donald Place, Elizabeth, New Jersey 07208 USA
Phone: (908)353-1655 Fax: (908)353-0255

Published simultaneously in Korea
by Hollym Corporation; Publishers
14-5 Kwanchol-dong, Chongno-gu, Seoul 110-111, Korea
Phone: (02)735-7554 Fax: (02)730-5149

Hard cover edition ISBN: 1-56591-006-0
Paperback edition ISBN: 1-56591-007-9
Library of Congress Catalog Card Number: 93-77111

Printed in Korea

Acknowledgments

In researching this book I certainly relied on, and owe a great deal to, some special sources which were most frequently a basis for some of the more general knowledge gathered. Also, for some of the information about the characters in this book, both the *Korea Herald* and the *Korea Times*, English language newspapers were indespensible. They both contained detailed records of many of the famous people either featured in special articles or related interviews. In addition, there are quite a few general histories which provided a basic, perspective of these characters. Among them:

Han, Woo-keun. *The History of Korea*. Honolulu: The University Press of Hawaii, 1980.

Henthorn, William E., *A History of Korea*. New York: The Free Press, 1971.

Hulbert's History of Korea. Edited by Clarence Norwood Weems. New York: Hillary House Publishers, Ltd., 1962.

Joe, Wanne J., *Traditional Korea: A Cultural History*. Seoul: Chungang University Press, 1972.

Lee, Ki-Baek. *A New History of Korea*. Cambridge: Harvard University Press, 1984.

Nahm, Andrew C., *Korea: Tradition and Transformation*. New Jersey: Hollym International Corp., 1988.

Rutt, Richard. *History of the Korean People*. Seoul: Royal Asiatic Society Korea Branch, 1972.

The following Korean language sources were helpful in obtaining some of the more obscure biographic information:

Encyclopedia of Korean History. Seoul: Dong-A Publishing Company, 1976.
Lee, Hyun-hee, *The History of People in Korea.* Korea: Chung Ah Publishing Company, 1987.

In addition, some very important persons were kind enough to talk with me about their direct experiences with some of the characters in this book. My thanks to Mr. Kim Shin (son of Kim Koo) who sat and told me stories of his father and helped focus my research. Kim Shin is famous in his own right and could arguably be included in such a book. Thanks to Yi T'ae-yong (wife of Hong Nanp'a), who consented to an interview and shared many facts and special moments between her and her husband. Lastly, I would like to thank Kong Tok-kwi (wife of Yun Po-son), who graciously provided an interview and a tour of the wonderful home of her and her husband, still located in Seoul. Their help added much to my research and my personal enrichment about the history of Korea.

I would also like to thank a few people who spent a lot of their personal time assisting me. Miss O Kyong-won, local librarian, had a genuine interest in this study and helped locate many important research documents for me. Also, Mr. Pak Chin-chol, devoted much of his personal time assisting me and helping ensure accurate translation when needed. I also thank my friend Mr. Ch'oe Chong-dae, a consultant for the Ch'ondogyo Church, who helped review the chapter on Ch'oe Che-u for accuracy and relevance.

There are many other kind people who helped along the way. Many I met while traveling around the peninsula visiting the various museums, shrines, birthplaces, etc., related to these characters. Many people went out of their way to help including government officials at local city halls, caretakers, and just common people who, through their kindness, helped me gather and focus my writings.

Finally, and most importantly, I want to thank my wife Yong, and my sons Nick and Matthew, for supporting me over the entire period it took to complete this project. All the time I didn't spend with them can never be replaced and their encouragement during the toughest of times helped me complete the task when I thought it might be impossible. Also, thanks to all my friends, who, with their kind words and help, also provided needed encouragement to allow me to persevere.

Richard Saccone

Contents

Acknowledgments   v
Introduction   xiii

I. POLITICIANS   1
1. Chang Myon (장 면)   3
2. Chun Doo-hwan (전 두환)   7
3. Kim Dae-jung (김 대중)   12
4. Kim Young-sam (김 영삼)   16
5. Park Chung-hee (박 정희)   21
6. Rhee Syng-man (이 승만)   25
7. Roh Tae-woo (노 태우)   29
8. Yi Ha-ung (이 하웅)   34
9. Yun Po-son (윤 보선)   39

II. KINGS AND QUEENS   43
10. King Kojong (고종)   45
11. King Sejong (세종)   49
12. Queen Sondok (선덕여왕)   54
13. Wang Kon (왕 건)   58
14. Yi Song-gye (이 성계)   62

III. MILITARY   67
15. Ch'oe Yong (최 영)   69

16. Kang Kam-ch'an (강 감찬) 74
17. Kim Yu-shin (김 유신) 79
18. Kyebaek (계백) 83
19. Ulchi Mundok (을지문덕) 87
20. Yi Sun-shin (이 순신) 92

IV. PHILOSOPHERS 97
21. Wonhyo (원효) 99
22. Yi Hwang (이 황) 103
23. Yi Yi (이 이) 107

V. RELIGIOUS FIGURES 111
24. Han Yong-un (한 용운) 113
25. Kim Tae-gon (김 대건) 117
26. Samyongdang (사명당) 121

VI. BUSINESSMEN 127
27. Chung Ju-yung (정 주영) 129
28. Kim Woo-choong (김 우중) 134

VII. SCHOLARS 139
29. Chi Sok-yong (지 석영) 141
30. Ch'oe Che-u (최 제우) 145
31. Ch'oe Ch'i-won (최 치원) 149
32. Chong In-bo (정 인보) 153
33. Chong Mong-ju (정 몽주) 156
34. Chong Yak-yong (정 약용) 161
35. Kim Chong-hui (김 정희) 165
36. Pang Chong-hwan (방 정환) 170

VIII. ARTISTS, WRITERS, PUBLISHERS, COMPOSERS 175
37. Ahn Eak-tay (안 익태) 177

38. Hong Nanp'a　(홍 난파) 182
39. Kim Song-su　(김 성수) 187
40. Shin Saimdang　(신 사임당) 191
41. Yi Kwang-su　(이 광수) 195

IX. PATRIOTS (Independence Fighters) 199
42. Ahn Ch'ang-ho　(안 창호) 201
43. Ahn Chung-gun　(안 중근) 205
44. Kim Koo　(김 구) 209
45. Kim Ok-kyun　(김 옥균) 213
46. Shin Ch'ae-ho　(신 채호) 217
47. So Chae-p'il　(서 재필) 221
48. Yi Sang-jae　(이 상재) 226
49. Yu Kwan-sun　(유 관순) 230
50. Yun Pong-gil　(윤 봉길) 235

Index 240

Introduction

Korea is a proud country with a very long and interesting history. For years it was almost unknown to Westerners as it was isolated by choice. In modern history, its occupation under the Japanese, for thirty-five years, further detracted from the interest and ability of Westerners to know much about its past.

More recently, Korea has become a significant player in both world politics and business. There is an increased interest in knowledge of Korea's past, culture and lifestyle. Many more people are visiting Korea, whether for business or tourism, and the more frequently they visit the deeper they probe for information about this wonderful and interesting land.

Much has been published about famous places in Korean history. There are many tourist guides and history books that detail these places. Conversely, relatively little is written about the people in Korean history. Even though their stories are diverse and interesting it is difficult for many foreigners to learn much about them. Not enough is written of such people in English and few foreigners read Korean well enough to decipher the often complex stories of their background. What little material is available in English is scattered and sometimes difficult to obtain. Much of it was written in the 1970's or earlier and is now out of print. It requires considerable effort just to obtain some of the materials that would provide an interested reader with the basic details of many historical characters of Korea.

This book is intended for those who are interested in Korea and desire a broad but brief knowledge of famous and/or common names of Korea. The fifty notable figures featured in this text are, not necessarily, all the most famous or the most important nor are they rank ordered. The names chosen were the result of a survey conducted by the author in 1991. Koreans from a variety of backgrounds were given a list of famous names and asked to pick fifty which they thought foreigners should study if they wanted to develop a basic knowledge of Korea. No doubt opinions will differ as to whether the list omitted someone of higher stature or included someone whose popularity is controversial. However, to know the names and backgrounds of those in this book will undoubtedly provide a diverse and respectable knowledge of Korea. There are names from many periods of history from Korea's Three Kingdoms to the present. Included are political figures, businessmen, religious figures, philosophers, journalists, kings, scholars, military figures and artists.

The information provided is concise. The first paragraph of each section provides a summary of why the individual is well known. Following that is more detailed information about the individual's life. The last paragraph includes famous places one may visit to learn more about the person.

It is my hope that curious minds will read this book and increase their interest in Korea. I hope people will use the book as a reference whenever they encounter famous names and wish to quickly become conversant in the basis of their popularity. I also hope this book will spur interest in visiting the many interesting locations associated with these famous persons and be used by those locations to help enlighten visitors at these attractions.

Note on Korean names: All names are given in Oriental fashion with family name first, given name then middle name, unless otherwise noted. A hyphen is inserted between given and middle names.

Many Koreans use the lunar calendar for important

dates such as birthdays, anniversaries, etc. All dates listed are of the solar calendar unless otherwise noted. Sometimes both dates are provided to clarify confusion one may encounter in finding different dates listed in different sources. It is sometimes important to know the actual date and corresponding calendar if one is interested in searching for events which occur on certain anniversaries, etc. Knowing the correct date will make it easier to keep current on future seminars or festivals, etc., which often occur at that time.

The terms South Korea, Republic of Korea and Korea are used interchangeably throughout. North Korea is only referred to specifically as such.

Spelling Guide for Korean Words

All Korean words are Romanized as they are pronounced, with the exception of proper nouns. Personal names such as Rhee Syng-man, and Kim Koo, etc., are spelled as the person or official representatives desired. Kim Koo for example, may sometimes appear in other publications as Kim Ku, but the *Kim* family and the Kim Koo Association, in Seoul, prefer Koo and I defered to their wishes. In all such cases I have complied with similar preferences. Names of commercial firms or universities were dealt with in a similar manner.

Names of cities and provinces were rendered in a form believed most easy for a foreigner to understand. For example, Kyongsangbukdo appears in this text as North Kyongsang Province. In Korean, *buk* meaning north, and *do* meaning province, were translated into English and arranged in the order most familiar to English speaking foreigners. Another example, Chejudo Island, appears in this text as Cheju Island as *do* in this case means island in Korean and to list it twice would be redundant.

I believe this system is more convenient than the traditional McCune-Reischauer system and more conducive to understanding by general readers.

I

POLITICIANS

Chang Myon

Chun Doo-hwan

Kim Dae-jung

Kim Young-sam

Park Chung-hee

Rhee Syng-man

Roh Tae-woo

Yi Ha-ung

Yun Po-son

1
Statesman and Political Leader

Chang Myon
(JOHN M. CHANG, 1899-1966)

Educator turned politician Chang was thrust into politics, in a sense, before he knew it. Chang is most remembered as Prime Minister in the second republic after the overthrow of President Rhee (1960) and up until his own ouster after the coup of, then general, Park Chung-hee (1961). While his intentions appeared righteous and his integrity was unquestioned, he could not seem to garner enough support from the populace to govern effectively. In the end he allowed himself to be shouldered from office by a more forceful military leadership.

Chang was born in the port city of Inch'on. He graduated from high school in 1917 in the city of Suwon, south of Seoul. He then attended an English language program at the YMCA in Seoul until 1919. Chang traveled to the U.S. to study and graduated from Manhattan College in New York in 1925. Upon returning to Korea he lived in Pyongyang and was involved in Catholic church matters there. He returned to Seoul in 1931, as principal of a boys' school and remained there until the close of World War II.

After the war, the U.S. military government in Korea

4 / KOREANS TO REMEMBER

Chang Myon, Prime Minister of the Second Republic of Korea

18 May, 1961, press conference announcing his departure from politics

was looking for bright people to serve in government. In 1946, Chang was appointed to the Interim Legislative Assembly created by the U.S. military to jump-start the self governing process in Korea. This body was composed of forty five elected and forty five appointed members. Chang was selected as an intelligent and capable man who had been educated in the U.S. and could contribute to the political process. He grew to fulfill those expectations and become an important member of the Assembly. He was soon elevated to prominence when he was appointed to head the three man committee that appeared before the United Nations general assembly to address the problem of Korea. As a result, the United Nations later formed a temporary commission to observe and facilitate elections in Korea. The elections were held on 10 May, 1948 and Chang was one of the representatives elected to set up the first government of South Korea. This National Assembly wrote the first constitution and then elected Rhee Syng-man the first president.

Rhee soon formed his administration and appointed Chang to one of the most important positions; Ambassador to the United States. He served effectively in the U.S. and received a Ph.D. from Fordham University during his tenure in Washington D.C. Shortly after the Korean War which began in June 1950, Chang returned to Korea and, by November 1951, was appointed Prime Minister by President Rhee and joined the government which was taking sanctuary in Pusan during the war. However, Chang resigned in April 1952 when he perceived a real chance to be nominated as a presidential candidate in the 1952 elections.

Although he did not receive the nomination in 1952 he did appear as an opposition party vice-presidential candidate against President Rhee and his candidate for vice-president, Yi Ki-bung. Rhee won the presidential election but Chang beat Yi in the vice presidential race. Rhee, feeling betrayed by Chang's decision to challenge his former sponsor, moved to limit Chang's power in government. Matters turned ugly on 28 September, 1956, when a pro-Rhee follower attempted to assassinate Chang in Seoul. He succeeded only in wounding Chang's hand. Chang was defeated by a Rhee and Yi ticket in 1960, after some very suspect elections. Soon after the elections, widespread demonstrations forced Rhee from office and an interim government was formed. Yun Po-son became president and Chang found himself elected Prime Minister. In this new government the power of the president had been reduced almost to ceremony and the Prime Minister held most of the power and responsibility. Chang's administration was plagued by factionalism, indecision and weak leadership. Between September 1960 and May 1961 Chang modified his cabinet three times still without significant gains in effectiveness or popularity. He was attempting to construct long term plans, when in May 1961, he was forced from office by the military coup of General Park Chung-hee. Chang was arrested and banned from political activity. He spent most of the remainder of his life in seclusion in his home.

In his later years, Chang suffered from liver trouble and was treated for hepatitis at several hospitals in Seoul. Finally in June 1966, he died just hours after arriving home in Myongnyun-dong, Seoul. He was buried at a Catholic cemetery in P'och'on-gun less than fifty kilometers north of Seoul after a large funeral service at Seoul Stadium followed by a procession through the streets of the capital attended by thousands of well-wishers.

Chang left a legacy of integrity in politics. He was respected by many for his contributions to democracy and his service to Korea.

2
Fifth President of Korea

Chun Doo-hwan
(1931-)

Military leader, politician and fifth President of the Republic of Korea, Chun emerged at a critical point in Korea's history and helped change its course. Although he may have shouldered his way into the presidency he presided over an administration born in turmoil but still managed to record some impressive economic gains for his country. Although opposed by many, he arranged the first peaceful transfer of power to a new president in modern Korea.

His family background was somewhat ordinary. Born as the sixth of nine children on 18 January, 1931, he grew up in a farming family in Hapch'on-gun, South Kyongsang Province. The Japanese occupation was in full swing during his childhood. Although his father tutored him in the Confucian classics, the Chun family moved to Taegu in time for Chun to attend elementary school there until 1945. He later graduated from a technical high school in 1951. With the Korean War already in progress, Chun entered the Korean Military Academy, in Chinhae, in 1951. He graduated in 1955, as part of the famous eleventh class, which was the first to complete the newly instituted four-year program modeled after the

Chun Doo-hwan, the 5th president of Korea

Chun Doo-hwan, 1 September, 1980 Inauguration, with his predecessor Ch'oe Kyu-ha, the 4th president of Korea attending

military academy at West Point. The old academy was modeled in the Japanese style and was only a two year program.

Chun then began a twenty-five year military career which ended with a coup, a rapid rise to power and ultimately the presidency. His first duties as a young officer included field duty as a platoon leader followed by training assignments which included the psychological warfare course of the U.S. Special Forces. He received additional training in the U.S. in 1960 at the U.S. Army Infantry School. Chun received a key assignment in 1961. After the overthrow of President Rhee, Chun was appointed as, then General, Park Chung-Hee's secretary of domestic affairs while Park was Chairman of the Supreme Council for National Reconstruction. Although only a captain, Chun held this position from September 1961 to August 1962 and enjoyed frequent exposure to the would-be president. He soon received other key posts leading up to his promotion to Commander of a battalion in the Capital Garrison Command in 1967. This proved fortunate as he could claim credit for annihilating a thirty-one man North Korean commando team which had infiltrated South Korea to kill President Park in January 1968. The following year, in December, Chun was appointed as the senior aid to the ROK Army Chief of Staff. Chun continued to receive key assignments critical to a successful career. Chun was promoted to colonel and made commander of a regiment in the famous White Horse division fighting in Vietnam in late 1970. While there he received a U.S. Bronze Star for his service. Chun returned to Korea in another command position until being chosen as a senior staff officer in the Presidential Security Force. In this position Chun again had frequent exposure to President Park who reportedly treated him very well. By January 1978, he was promoted to brigadier general and reassigned to the 1st Infantry Division where he was commended by President Park when Chun's men discovered a North Korean infiltration tunnel under the Demilitarized Zone. Chun received his second star and probably his most important assignment as commander of the Defense Security Command in March

1979. It was from this position that he launched into action when President Park was suddenly assassinated on 26 October of the same year by his CIA chief Kim Jae-gyu. Chun took charge of the investigation and arrested the martial law commander for complicity in the assassination sometime later on 12 December, 1979. This resulted in some bloodshed and caused Chun to seize control of the military and "retire" many high ranking officers. The following April, acting president Ch'oe Kyu-ha appointed Chun director of the CIA which offered Chun additional breadth of power.

Student demonstrations had been increasing due to the authoritarian political maneuvers in motion. In May 1980, however, things took a serious turn for the worst. When some leading opposition figures were arrested demonstrations erupted nationwide with the most serious in Kwangju City. The city was virtually taken over and military troops were used to restore order. Their methods were somewhat brutal and at least 190 people were killed. This bloody episode would not be shaken by Chun the rest of his political career.

In the next few months things changed rapidly. Chun was promoted to four star general retired from the military and was elected president in August. Over the next few months a new constitution was accepted, political activity was again authorized and, in February, President Chun was reelected as president for a single seven year term. This began what is known as the fifth republic.

President Chun quickly launched his economic and social programs for the country. He successfully obtained the authorization in 1981, to host the 1988 Summer Olympics in Seoul and started a major construction effort to rebuild the nation. His administration was successful in achieving economic growth and holding down inflation. Relations with North Korea continued to be a problem, however, and on 9 October, 1983, disaster struck. On the second day of Chun's state visit to Burma, North Korean commandos blew up the platform where Chun was to speak, killing twenty-one people including four of his cabinet members. Chun was late for the ceremony and narrowly escaped injury. Domestic political problems, scandals, and the "ghost" of Kwangju also continued to haunt his administration. In 1987, his successor, Roh Tae-woo was elected and Chun stepped down as president soon after. He soon went into self-imposed exile at a Buddhist temple in Sorak Mountain to allow some political healing within Korea. He returned to his home in Yonhi-dong, Seoul in December 1990 and is attempting to lead a quiet life there.

3
Perennial Opposition Politician

Kim Dae-jung
(1924-)

Prominent politician, businessman, perennial opposition leader and presidential candidate, Kim Dae-jung is a noted and often controversial figure that has made a permanent impression on the political history of Korea. His politics have often brought him in conflict with the government of South Korea and his activities have often brought him headlines both at home and abroad.

He was born to a farming family on the island of Hauido off the southwestern coast of Korea, on 6 January as the second of seven children. Later his family moved to the mainland coastal city of Mokp'o. Kim graduated at the top of his class at a high school in Mokp'o in 1943. He later studied for his master's degree in economics, in Seoul, at Kyunghee University. Between high school and college he went to work for a freight shipping company. He did so well that after a few years he became the head of his own company eventually owning nine small freighters. In 1950, he became president of a daily newspaper in Mokp'o. He happened to be in Seoul in June of that year at the start of the Korean War. Kim, determined to reach his home, spent fifteen days walking

Kim Dae-jung, perennial presidential candidate and prominent opposition party leader

back to Mokp'o. When he finally arrived he was arrested by the North Koreans but was one of the fortunate few who managed to escape.

After the war, Kim made a few unsuccessful bids for a National Assembly seat losing three elections. He became the official spokesman for Prime Minister Chang Myon for the brief period following the forced resignation of President Rhee Syng-man in 1960.

Kim finally realized his dream and won a National Assembly seat in May of 1961 just two days before Park Chung-hee staged a coup, took over the government and dissolved the Assembly. He was one of many political figures who were arrested at that time. In 1963, he was released, and when the political process was resumed, he won a decisive victory to another assembly seat as a Mokp'o representative. He was reelected in another landslide in 1967. Kim continued to consolidate his political strength and became the surprise candidate of the New Democratic Party in the 1971 presidential elections. The election was very close. Even though there were seven candidates Kim received approximately 46 percent of the vote. There were major suspicions and allegations of election fraud but, even in defeat, Kim was propelled into the height of political notoriety. Kim continued his opposition politics and criticism of the government. Later that year Kim was involved in an automobile accident that left him with injuries he suffers with even today. It was later reportedly admitted that the accident was part of a government assassination attempt on Kim's life. Following the accident he was kept under frequent surveillance and his political activities were limited.

Kim was in Japan when President Park declared martial law in 1972, and initiated his new Yushin constitution. Kim would not return to Korea because he knew he would be unable to carry on his political career under the restrictions of martial law. He continued to speak out against the Park regime from Japan. In August 1973, he was kidnapped from a Tokyo hotel room and brought back to Korea. Kim stated he was drugged and beaten and put aboard a ship and thought he was to be killed. He was spared death somehow but returned to Korea under house arrest.

This did not deter Kim much, however, in March 1976, Kim and some other noted citizens signed a letter encouraging President Park to restore democratic processes and resign. Kim was arrested and later given an eight year prison term for agitating to overthrow the government. Kim was released in December of 1978 after serving about thirty-three months of his sentence. Although his sentence was suspended due to ill health Kim was still under tight restrictions to refrain from political activity. After the 1979 assassination of President Park, Kim decided to resume his political activity. He declared his hope to run for president. In May 1980, violent demonstrations broke out in Kwangju in southwestern Korea. On 16 May Kim was arrested on charges of mass agitation. The demonstrations in Kwangju turned into rebellion and many people were killed when troops were used to restore order. Kim was tried in connection with the rebellion and in September was sentenced to death by hanging. President Chun Doo-hwan later reduced his sentence to twenty years just before the president traveled to the U.S. to meet President Reagan. Fortunately for Kim, he was released in December 1982 under an agreement that he leave Korea. Kim went to the U.S. and received medical treatment in Washington D.C. before accepting a fellowship at Harvard. Kim decided to return to Korea in 1985 even though the Chun government confined him to his home. He was a serious presidential contender again in 1987 coming in a close third. Kim also made a valiant run for the Presidency in 1992 coming in second.

Kim is a devout Catholic. He has been married to Lee Hee-ho since 1962. His first wife died in 1959. He has three sons, two from his first marriage and one from his second.

Whatever the future holds Kim has already made his mark on the political history of Korea. He has been a force to be reckoned with in the drive for democracy for almost thirty years.

4
Consummate Politician and Seventh President of Korea

Kim Young-sam
(1927-)

Regardless of one's political orientation, Kim is one of the most famous political figures in modern Korea. His political career touches five decades and he has distinguished himself as a national political party leader and National Assembly member. Previously most famous as an opposition politician and perennial presidential candidate, Kim has helped shape the political face of Korea and has significantly contributed to the nation's move toward democracy. He finally reached his ultimate goal when he was elected president in 1992.

The beautiful island of Koje, near the south coast port city of Pusan, was Kim's birthplace on 20 December, 1927. Kim was the only son of six children and his father, Kim Hong-jo, was a fisherman and operated some fishing vessels in the area. His youth was shaped during the last years of the Japanese colonial period and he graduated from Kyongnam High School two years after the end of World War II.

Accepted into the prestigious Seoul National University, Kim began his studies and was able to complete a Bachelor

Kim Young-sam, 25 February, 1993 7th President of Korea

of Arts in Philosophy in 1952, despite the interruption of the Korean War, during which he became a troop information and education specialist in the Student Volunteer Corps. That same year he married Sohn Myong-sun, a student of Ewha Womans University, who he met during his college years.

After graduation, he quickly began preparing for his political career and won his first election in 1954, making him a National Assembly member at the early age of twenty seven. He was an active assemblyman through the years of President Rhee's administration and spent much time developing his strong political base in the Pusan and South Kyongsang Province area.

During the fall of the Rhee government in 1960 and the subsequent coup and takeover by then general, Park Chung-hee, Kim became an ardent opposition leader, which would bring him much trouble over the next eighteen years of the Park administration. In fact, he was arrested in 1962 and imprisoned for his opposition to the Park government. He continued speaking out however and, for the duration of the Park regime, he preached his politics in foreign countries wherever he could find an audience. In 1964, he traveled to Europe, Southeast Asia and the Middle East. Two years later, he went to Illinois as a guest of the Chicago Trade Association and in 1968, he attended both the Republican and Democratic National Conventions in the United States. The following year brought a key constitutional change which allowed President Park to run for a third term. This measure was very controversial and stirred opposition party members and student activists into action. Kim's opposition activities caused him to be physically attacked with nitric acid, reportedly by a government intelligence agent. Kim continued his opposition and was elected president of the New Democratic Party in 1974 and 1979. Again however, in 1979, his opposition to the Park administration caused him to be suspended from his duties as party president, and expelled from the National Assembly in early October, which caused massive demonstrations in his home province. By the end of October, political turmoil had escalated to serious levels and President Park was assassinated.

A new military coup was completed in December by then general, Chun Doo-hwan, and when demonstrations in Kwangju erupted in May 1980, Kim and other leaders were arrested. Kim continued under house arrest until the end of April 1981, and was banned from political activities. From 31 May, 1981 he was placed under house arrest for the next two years during which time he went on a hunger strike for 23 days in May 1983, calling for democratic reform. Even while under a political ban he organized the New Korea Democratic Party (NKDP) in 1985 which rapidly gained popularity and posed great political problems for the ruling party during the general elections in February of that year. The NKDP won 29.2 percent of the vote while the ruling party won a meager 35.3 percent. In many large cities, including Seoul, the NKDP actually won more of the popular vote than the ruling party.

The following month his political ban was lifted and he continued his quest for political reform until he was eventually elected president of the Reunification Democratic Party in 1987, the same year he ran for president.

The presidential race of 1987 was fast paced and exiting. The three Kims, (Kim Young-sam, Kim Dae-jung, and Kim Jong-pil) were all in the campaign against the ruling Democratic Justice Party candidate Roh Tae-woo. All the candidates drew large crowds and much emotion, repressed during years without a popular election, precipitated into violence, in some cases cutting short some of the campaign rallies. In the end, the two leading opposition candidates split the opposition vote allowing Roh to win the election with over 8.2 million votes to Kim's 6.3 million votes. Kim Dae-jung and Kim Jong-pil took third and fourth place with 6.1 million and 1.8 million votes respectively.

The years following have seen Kim continue in popularity and even move toward moderation and reconciliation. On 22 January, 1990, Kim merged his opposition party with the ruling party to form the Democratic Liberal Party. The party created four leading posts of which Kim was given the spot as Executive Chairman. From this position Kim campaigned and was elected president in 1992. Kim has permanently etched his place in Korea's politcal history as a man with a say in the political development of his country and the resolve to overcome whatever obstacles prevent the accomplishment of his goals.

5
Strong Leader and Third President of Korea

Park Chung-hee
(1917-1979)

Park Chung-hee was the third president of the Republic of Korea. He replaced the second republic in a bloodless coup in May 1961, and became president some two years later in 1963. Before that he was a primary school teacher and eventually a military general. His terms as president were marked by significant economic gains but also included political and social repressions. He was finally assassinated in 1979, by his CIA chief.

Park was born in Sonsan-gun, North Kyongsang Province, in southeastern Korea, about 30 miles north of Taegu, on 30 September, 1917. Park's Korean name is more closely pronounced Pak, not "pack." It was written in English as Park to more closely coincide with the English pronunciation of the name. Park was educated in Taegu and eventually obtained a teaching license and taught at the Munkyong Primary School from 1937 to 1940.

Park decided to embark on a military career and entered the Manchukuo Military Academy in 1940 for two years. He graduated at the top of his class and proceeded to the Japanese Imperial Military Academy for their advanced

LEFT Park Chung-hee, the 3rd President of Korea   BOTTOM With his wife Yook Yong-soo at the Presidential residence on New Year's Day 1973

course. He had attained the rank of first lieutenant in the Japanese Army by the end of World War II. After the war he entered the Korean Military Academy, and upon completion of the advanced course, was commissioned a captain in 1946. In 1948, he reportedly took part in a revolt with other junior officers who were opposed to the division of the Korean peninsula. Park was sentenced to death but was later restored to rank and pardoned. Park rose to brigadier general in 1953 during the Korean War. He then traveled to the United States to attend the advanced course at the U.S. Army Artillery School in Fort Sill, Oklahoma. He returned to Korea and held several posts before being promoted to major general in 1958. On 16 May, 1961, Major General Park led the bloodless coup that took over the government from the second republic. Park was promoted to lieutenant general in August 1961 and shortly after was promoted to full general in November. Park left the military in August 1963 in order to accept the nomination for the presidency. He was elected president on 16 October of that year and was inaugurated on 17 December, 1963.

President Park's first term initiated what later became known as the Korean economic miracle. His export-oriented economy marked significant gains in the South Korean standard of living. Politically, Park took some bold risks by normalizing relations with Japan in 1965 and sending troops to fight as U.S. allies in Vietnam. Over 350,000 Korean troops rotated through Vietnam from 1965-73 gaining valuable combat experience. Some 3,050 South Korean troops were killed during the Vietnam War.

President Park was reelected in May 1967, was sworn in and started his second term on 1 July of that same year. North Korea had been accused of various provocations against the South up to this period. However in January 1968, a thirty-one man commando team infiltrated across the DMZ and worked their way into Seoul with a mission to kill President Park. They reached within 1,000 yards of the presidential mansion. A firefight ensued and all but one of the commando team were killed and many South Koreans died defending the president. One member of the team was captured and revealed details of the mission. Later that month the U.S. ship, Pueblo, was seized by North Korea in international waters off Wonsan.

In April 1971, Park was reelected but narrowly defeated the opposition candidate Kim Dae-jung. President Park was working hard establishing South Korea in the world community. By December 1972, President Park had expanded diplomatic relations by signing treaties with 60 nations. This brought the total number of nations which had such relations with South Korea to 77. Domestically however, Park was having serious difficulty. Despite economic gains Park's efforts to control political power were causing much dissent. Park was able to institute a new constitution, Yushin, which means revitalizing reform. Yushin gave the president additional powers including the ability to issue emergency decrees. To the dismay of many, Park issued four such decrees in 1974. In August of the same year, a gunman tried to assassinate Park during a speech at the National Theater in Seoul. The gunman missed the president but killed his wife, Yook Yong-soo. In 1978, in spite of continuous political difficulties, the National Conference for Unification reelected him for six more years. This seemingly endless rule caused more political turmoil. Opposition pressure and student demonstrations mounted through 1979. In March, the arrests of perennial opposition candidate Kim Dae-jung, former president Yun Po-son, and religious dissident leader Ham Sok-hon incited additional political instability. In October, student demonstrations broke out which resulted in violent police actions and the declaration of martial law. On 26 October Park was assasinated by his CIA chief, Kim Chae-kyu as they had dinner. His death precipitated more turmoil which eventually led to another coup and allowed another military man to become president.

Despite his authoritarian rule Park is remembered as a man who accomplished so much for Korea. He is buried at the National Cemetery in southern Seoul.

6
First President of Korea
Rhee Syng-man
(Unam, 1875 -1965)

Rhee Syng-man is famous as an independence fighter and politician. He is most famous as the first president of the Republic of Korea. Rhee was president for twelve years which were some of the most tumultuous in the country's modern history. Rhee's administration weathered the Korean War but could not withstand political controversy that finally brought down the president amidst student demonstrations. Rhee fled to Hawaii where he lived in exile until his death.

Rhee Syng-man (Rhee is the family name) was born in Hwanghae Province Korea on 26 April, 1875. When his older brother died in childhood he became the sixth successive generation of only sons. When Rhee was nine years old he was stricken during an epidemic of smallpox which left him blind in both eyes. His family tried many traditional remedies and herb doctors but could not cure the boy. As a last resort, a relative suggested Rhee's father take him to a Western doctor who was living in Korea at the time. The doctor, a Presbyterian minister, Horace Allen, cured the boy within a few days. Rhee would develop a keen interest in the

ABOVE Rhee Syng-man receiving Ph.D. at Princeton in June 1910   RIGHT With his wife Francesca on honeymoon trip to Hawaii in October 1934

Announcing the establishment of the new Republic of Korea government in August 15, 1948

West and travel there to study and complete his education.

Rhee's childhood education was traditional. He studied the Chinese classics and mastered writing Chinese characters at an early age. At age nineteen he joined the Paejae School which was run by Methodist missionaries and taught a more Western curriculum. This school sparked Rhee's interest in English which later helped him complete his education in the West.

Rhee attended Paejae and learned from another young reformer, So Chae-p'il, who had studied in America. So Chae-p'il formed a discussion group there called the Mutual Friendship Society. In 1896, the group moved away from the school and became famous under the name The Independence Club. Rhee was very active in the club but events that year significantly changed his life. Rhee took part in a failed coup attempt to overthrow the pro-Japanese government which made Rhee a wanted man. Rhee persisted in agitation through The Independence Club and was arrested and imprisoned from 1898-1904. After enduring terrible beatings and torture he was released and went to the United States to study.

Rhee entered George Washington University in 1905 under a scholarship. He graduated there in 1907, started postgraduate work at Harvard University and received his master's degree in 1908. Rhee decided to do additional graduate work at Princeton and while there attracted the attention of the president of Princeton who at that time was none other than Woodrow Wilson. He received his doctorate from Princeton in 1910, the same year Japan annexed Korea. Rhee was the first Korean to receive a Ph.D. from a U.S. university.

Rhee helped form a provisional government in Seoul in 1919. The government was later moved and functioned from Shanghai during the rest of the Japanese occupation. Rhee was elected president of this government in exile, but spent most of this period in the United States lobbying for Korean independence as Korea's American representative. After twenty years at this post Rhee lost the presidency of the government in exile to those reformers centered in Shanghai.

Rhee, however, continued to spend most of the war years in the United States lobbying for Korean independence until 1945.

At the close of World War II, Rhee returned to Korea well known to its liberators and fluent in English. Although aged he kept up his efforts and was elected president in 1948 at the age of seventy-three. He was reelected in 1952, 56, and 60. By the time he was reelected in 1956 he was the oldest head of state in the world at eighty-one. His highly centralized form of government was noted for its efficiency and was often denigrated as a kind of one-man rule. Rhee's popularity had been waning in the later years of his administration. It was in 1960 that, what appeared to be tampered election results, prompted mass demonstrations which forced the resignation of Rhee. Following his resignation on 27 April, 1960, he went into exile in Hawaii and died there five years later.

Rhee married an Austrian, Francesca Donner in New York in 1934. Rhee was fifty-nine at the time and Donner was thirty-four. Francesca lived in their residence in Ihwadong, in northeastern Seoul until her death on 19 March, 1992, at the age of ninety-two. She was buried with her husband at the National Cemetery on 23 March, 1992. Their residence, known as Ihwajang, is open to the public and contains many historic photos and personal belongings of Rhee and his wife.

7
Master of Political Compromise
Roh Tae-woo
(1932-)

As the sixth president of the Republic of Korea, Roh's life story is fascinating. How he became president, however, is almost as interesting. His rise through the military, and into politics surprised many political observers who did not recognize him as a future leader of the country. He is probably most remembered for his history making, 29 June, 1987 speech, in which he consented to major changes in the government of South Korea just after announcing his candidacy for president. That speech and the developments resulting afterward, truly altered the democratic course of the country.

A small farming village near Taegu City, in North Kyongsang Province, was the birthplace of Roh on 4 December, 1932. His father, who worked in the local village office, died in an auto accident when Roh was still a young boy. He grew up partly during the end of the Japanese occupation of Korea which was in many ways the harshest period of their occupation. Sometime after liberation he was fortunate enough to be sent to a prestigious high school by a helpful relative. Kyongbuk High School was not only a good school but its students often had gone on to important posi-

The 6th President of Korea Roh Tae-woo

Roh Tae-woo and U.S. President George Bush making a toast

tions later in life. The socialization during this period is culturally important and friends made during this time are often friends for life. His high school years were important for Roh for it was then that he met and became friends with Chun Doo-hwan (see chapter 2). This relationship with the future fifth president undoubtedly helped him climb the ladder of military and political success.

After the Korean War erupted in 1950, Roh joined the army and was later admitted to the Korean Military Academy as was his friend Chun. They both graduated in 1955, in what is now the famous eleventh class, which was the first class to complete the full four year program. Throughout their military careers the two men supported each other especially when they were needed most.

In the military, Roh began with some key assignments which helped him progress through the ranks. Along the way, he traveled to the US for training at the Special Warfare school at Fort Bragg, North Carolina, and was promoted to battalion commander in Vietnam, in the famous Tiger Division. He returned to Korea in 1974 to command the Airborne Special Warfare Brigade, and by 1979, had become the division commander of Korea's elite First Division.

That year was critical to Roh and the entire country. In October, President Park Chung-hee was assassinated and by December, Chun, then head of the Defense Security Command, led a coup and took control of the military. His friend, Roh, was ordered to arrest Chun, but instead sent troops to support him, ultimately making the difference in the coup's success. Later when Chun ultimately consolidated his power and became president, Roh's career continued to profit. Chun later appointed Roh the head of the Defense Security Command and rose quickly to four star rank by the time he retired from military life in 1981.

Choosing politics as a civilian career, Roh quickly rotated through some key political posts in the Chun administration. He was first made Minister of Political Affairs in 1981, followed by Minister of Sports in 1982, and Minister of Home Affairs that same year. The following year, however, he formally left the Chun administration to take an important post as head of the Seoul Olympic Organizing Committee. In this job he gained respect as an efficient and capable administrator and all along remained as a close confidant to the president. He emerged as a powerful man in Korea and a trusted advisor to the Chun administration and in 1985 became the head of the ruling Democratic Justice Party. Roh was skillful in helping the Chun administration but was put to his greatest test within two years.

The beginning of 1987 brought severe problems for the government. Student demonstrations were becoming more intense and increasingly more violent. Opposition leaders were demanding radical reform in the government and many were unsure if Chun would allow the peaceful transfer of power as promised by the end of that year. Chun's decision to suspend political talks on constitutional revision precipitated a serious political crisis. By the time Roh was elected the party's candidate for president, that June, the country was paralyzed with demonstrations.

While being close to Chun had helped him rise to power, many people complained that the administration was trying to replace one dictator with another, and Roh now found the relationship carried some political baggage that could hinder his future success. But Roh surprised his country and the world on 29 June when he announced sweeping changes to the government and submitted to most of the opposition demands for change almost completely removing the wind from the political sails of the opposition. He restored opposition leader Kim Dae-jung's civil rights, agreed to direct election of the president, more freedom of the press and many other improvements. The election was still five months away at that time and Roh had to struggle through a strenuous campaign, but was finally elected president on 17 December with 36.9% of the vote.

His presidency witnessed the success of the 88 Olympics, which he helped organize, and although it had its rough spots his administration enjoyed some impressive successes. Completing his term in 1993, he will likely be remembered as the man who accelerated the democratic development of Korea.

8
Man of Vision and Intrigue

Yi Ha-ung
(Hungson Taewongun, 1820 –1898)

More commonly known as Taewongun, this conservative Regent ruled in his son's stead for ten years. To some he was a tyrant, and obstacle to progress, to others he was the preserver of Korean tradition and savior from foreign intruders. His rule was filled with controversy and political intrigue. He was eventually forced from his position and compelled to take refuge in China. The Taewongun was a key character in the political transformation of Korea in the late nineteenth century. A relative of the official Yi Dynasty lineage by adoption, not birth, Taewongun did not benefit from his royal connections much in his early life. He was schooled, as was common in that period, in the Chinese classics, and became proficient in painting and calligraphy. This did not net him the important government positions he desired, however. Reportedly, he was somewhat embarrassed by his low status and resented his less than honorable treatment from his relatives. He would someday rise to a position where he could repay their "kindness."

The year of his destiny was 1864. King Ch'olchong, the 25th king of the Yi Dynasty, died on 16 January of that year.

LEFT Hungson Taewongun, Yi Ha-ung   RIGHT Stone tablets with anti-Western slogans like this were placed throughout Korea during Taewongun's reign

Artillery used against French and American troops in 1866 and 1871

King Ch'olchong had no heir and had failed to designate a replacement. He left three widows, the oldest and most powerful of whom was Queen Shinjong. It was her privilege to determine the next ruler of Korea. She decided fairly quickly that Yi Myong-bok, second son of Yi Ha-ung (Taewongun), would become king. Queen Shinjong felt he was the most suitable male in line to replace the king. She had not lingered in her decision and appointed Yi Myong-bok, as the Prince of Iksong on the same day the king had died. Yi Myong-bok, who would later rule under the name of Kojong, was only twelve years old, too young to actually govern the kingdom. It was decided that Yi Ha-ung would rule as Kojong's regent. On 17 January Yi was given the honorary title Taewongun, meaning the father of a king.

Taewongun faced some serious problems as he became regent. The kingdom had been plagued by peasant uprisings, corruption, and serious financial difficulty. In addition, an international rivalry over Korea was growing among foreign powers, especially those adjacent to the peninsula. Taewongun was a reformer in the sense that he wanted to remold the traditional Yi Dynasty government structure and increase the power of the throne. At the same time he was violently anti-foreign, which quickly put him at odds with those who thought that aping many of the foreign methods was the most effective path to modernization. In order to reform the government bureaucracy he chose to dissolve a few of the many committees and councils that used to permeate the government. In doing so he broke more than a few rice bowls, which alienated the upper class and made him many enemies. In addition, he constantly had to contend with attacks on the legitimacy of his rule.

The 1860's saw an increase in Western contacts in Asia. This was in direct conflict with the philosophy that such contacts would only alter the social balance and disrupt the country. This fear was reinforced as missionaries began to convert large numbers of Koreans to Catholicism which did, in fact create conflict with many Confucian customs and principles. This prompted a major persecution of Catholics that resulted in the brutal deaths of thousands of the followers, and the execution of three fourths of the French priests in the country. This, in turn, precipitated a military reaction from the French which initially was troublesome but the small French force was eventually defeated and Taewongun's popularity rose somewhat. Other Western powers, including America, were soon knocking at the door and demanding a relationship with the kingdom. There was much division within the country on the political and economic direction of the government, including the best method to deal with foreigners.

The pro-Chinese Taewongun was confronted by the pro-Japanese faction led by Queen Min, wife of young King Kojong. By 1873, King Kojong was old enough to reign and the queen, who was two years older than Kojong and more politically astute, helped instigate the movement to force Taewongun into retirement. Ironically, the queen was hand-picked by Taewongun to become Kojong's wife some years before. She was from the same Min family as his own wife. He could not have foreseen that she would become one of his most potent enemies.

Even though he retired to his home in Yangju he remained a political force for many years. Later, in 1881, a rise in Japanese influence in Korea, prompted a plot to oust the Min faction and King Kojong and reinstate the Taewongun. By 1882, another anti-foreign wave swelled within the country. Riots erupted that included an attempt on the queen's life. Taewongun was asked to return to power to calm the masses, which he did. However, the Chinese wanting to ensure tranquility and guarantee their own influence in Korea, kidnapped Taewongun and took him to China. He was eventually allowed to return to Korea when the Chinese were satisfied the atmosphere was appropriate. He sustained some political influence throughout the remainder of his life. Taewongun had made some significant improvements during his relatively brief reign, however, his traditional political philosophy and dated economic positions were overcome by the world around him. His impression on Korea though, was such that the name "Taewongun", which had been given to many others in history, is most closely associated with him even today.

9
Respected Leader and Second President of Korea

Yun Po-son
(1897-1990)

Long time civil servant, legislator, politician, architect and opposition party leader, Yun is most famous as the president of South Korea during the Second Republic, from August 1960 until he resigned in March 1962. After being forced from office he became a hardened opposition leader and opposition presidential candidate.

Born in Asan, South Ch'ungch'ong Province, before the turn of the twentieth century, Yun experienced the late Yi Dynasty Korea for only the early years of his childhood. By the time he became a teenager Korea was annexed by the Japanese and Yun's early adult life was shaped during the Japanese colonial period. He was fortunate enough to travel outside Korea and attend college in Scotland where he graduated from Edinburgh University in 1930.

After World War II and the liberation of Korea, Yun was active in politics. After the formation of the Republic of Korea government in 1948, Yun was appointed mayor of Seoul and maintained the post until 1949 when he became the Minister of Commerce in the administration of President Rhee. He also held a position as president of the Korean Red

Yun Po-son, speaking to large crowds in Yosu during the 1967 presidential election
LEFT   Yun Po-son, the 2nd President of Korea

Cross in the years leading to his first position as an Assemblyman in 1954. Yun maintained an assembly seat until 1960, rising to the head of the Democratic Party in 1957. It was from this position that fate propelled him to his highest achievement when the collapse of the Rhee administration ultimately led him to the presidency in 1960.

The decade beginning in 1960 was one of change for both Yun and his country. The abuses of the previous decade under the Rhee administration peaked during the March 1960 presidential election. After some suspicious election practices by Rhee's Liberal Party and the alleged use of the National Police, military and other forces to ensure the election of his running mate, riots and demonstrations broke out nationwide. By 19 April the demonstrations had become paralyzing and after many student deaths and even more injuries, ultimately resulted in the overthrow of the government. President Rhee was exiled to Hawaii where he died some five years later.

After the adoption of a new constitution and the election of new representatives in July, the representatives elected Yun as the second president of Korea and Chang Myon (see chapter 1) as premier in August. Both men were respected for their knowledge and integrity but did not exert the strong leadership needed to steer the new government. Neither could garner the support of the people and various factions and special interests quickly formed, posing additional political problems for the government. In addition, corruption and unrest continued to grow until May the following year when Park Chung-hee (see chapter 5) carried out a successful coup bringing an end to the second republic. Yun resigned but was persuaded to stay on as president even though the country was ruled by a military junta. In March 1962, then General Park, established a new law restricting certain political activities which resulted in President Yun resigning from office.

Yun started his opposition politics shortly after, becoming the leader of the Civil Rule Party and preparing to run as a presidential candidate in the 1963 election. The October election was extremely close with Park edging Yun 4.7 million to 4.5 million votes, to become Korea's third president. Not altogether discouraged Yun's party merged with another smaller political party some two years later to form the Popular Party (Min Jung Dang). By the 1967 presidential election, Yun became the candidate of still another political party (New Democratic Party) but President Park significantly widened the margin of victory.

The 1967 election was Yun's last presidential bid. He was already seventy years old and had a distinguished political career. He did not retire from politics but went on to become the leader of the National Party (Kuk Min Dang) in 1970 and an advisor to the New Peoples Party (Shin Min Dang) in 1979.

Yun died on 23 July, 1990, at the age of ninety-three, in his home in Ankuk-dong, Chongno-gu, Seoul. He had been hospitalized at Seoul National University hospital for some time due to respiratory problems which developed into pneumonia. In addition, he reportedly suffered from high blood pressure and diabetes. He was buried in the family grave in his hometown. His birthplace was designated as a cultural property and may still be seen today. His house in Seoul still exists and is historic in its own right, but is no longer open to the public.

II

KINGS AND QUEENS

King Kojong

King Sejong

Queen Sondok

Wang Kon

Yi Song-gye

10
Korea's Last King

King Kojong
(1852-1919)

Kojong (Yi Myong-bok) was the 26th king of the Yi Dynasty. He became king in 1864 at the age of twelve. He reigned over the opening of Korea to the West and the decline and fall of the Yi Dynasty (1392-1910).

Kojong was born as the second son of Yi Ha-ung, who was a direct descendant of Yi Myo, a son of the sixteenth Yi Dynasty king (King Injo, 1623-1649). Kojong became king after the death of King Ch'olchong who had no heir and had named no successor. Kojong was believed to be the most suitable male member of the Yi clan and so became king. Because of Kojong's youth, his father was appointed as Regent and given the title Taewongun (see chapter 8). In the first years of Kojong's reign the Taewongun tried vigorously to restore the prestige of the early Yi Dynasty. He began the reconstruction of Kyongbok Palace in Seoul and initiated the rearmament of Korea. Taewongun was forced out of power in 1873 by the family of Kojong's wife, Queen Min. The queen was two years older than Kojong and had much political acumen. Ironically she had been handpicked by Taewongun to be Kojong's wife.

Portrait of King Kojong

Picture of the royal family (King Kojong in the middle)

As Kojong assumed full power in 1874 he concluded some serious change was needed in how to deal with foreigners. Many Western countries and Japan were trying to force open relations with the very isolationist kingdom of Korea. Such efforts by Japan in the 1870's resulted in the Treaty of Kanghwa, in 1876, which was Korea's first modern diplomatic relationship. Developing rivalry among neighboring Russia, China and Japan over Korea gave Kojong great concern. Kojong sought to balance this mounting pressure by signing "The Treaty of Amity and Commerce" with the United States in May of 1882. The United States was the first Western nation to establish diplomatic relations with Korea. Other Western nations like Britain and Germany soon followed. Many Koreans disliked such relations with foreign countries, especially Japan, and believed the influence of those countries was too strong. In July of 1882, an anti-foreign wave resulted in a mob attack on the Japanese legation in Seoul leaving six Japanese dead and others injured. This resulted in disorder in the government, the return to power of the Taewongun, and the ultimate dispatch of Chinese and Japanese troops to Korea to reestablish control. King Kojong returned to power after the incident. China and Japan were both posturing to increase their influence over Korea. Kojong was supportive of reform and the import of Western technology to help strengthen Korea. Within the government however, division was deep. The Progressives, who wanted drastic reform along Japanese lines were losing ground to the conservatives who were more closely aligned with the Chinese. On 4 December, 1884, the Progressives staged a bloody palace coup aimed at breaking Korea's subservience to China and establishing a reform government under King Kojong. This incident, known as the Kapshin Coup, was initially successful and the Progressives were able to quickly form an administration. Within a few days however, Chinese troops attacked and trampled the coup killing many of its participants. Japan retaliated by sending troops and forcing Korea to pay an indemnity for damages caused during the fighting. Japan and China later negotiated the Li-Ito agreement, in 1885, which required both countries to withdraw troops and essentially stop interfering in Korea's internal affairs. The Sino-Japanese rivalry continued over Korea and ultimately resulted in the Sino-Japanese War of 1894-95. In October 1895 Queen Min was assassinated by a Japanese. Japan defeated the Chinese handily and increased their grip on Korea. Kojong instituted additional governmental reforms including the adoption of the Gregorian calendar, the establishment of modern elementary schools and other social changes. He also sought increased ties with Russia.

Russia's main objective was to remove Japanese influence in Korea, while the Japanese sought to eliminate the growing influence of Russia and finally consolidate their power in Korea. This rivalry subsequently developed into the Russo-Japanese War of 1904-5. Japan quickly defeated the Russians and declared Korea a protectorate. Korea's fate was sealed.

Kojong abdicated his throne on 22 June, 1907. His son, Sunjong, replaced him and was quickly sent to Japan to be educated. Japan annexed Korea in 1910 and began their brutal 35 year occupation. Kojong died on 22 January, some nine years later, amidst rumors he had been poisoned by the Japanese.

Kojong reigned during a turbulent transformation of Korea into the realities of the modern world. Unfortunately, he was overcome by those changes even as he helped develop them.

11
Sage King and Founder of the Written Language

King Sejong
(1397–1450)

King Sejong was one of the greatest and is one of the best known kings of Korea. He is celebrated as the inventor of the written Korean language, *han-gul*. He is remembered as a king concerned for his people and committed to their intellectual advancement.

On 15 May (10 April by the lunar calendar), 1397, Sejong was born as the third son to Prince Chong-an, the fifth son of T'aejo, the founder of the Yi Dynasty. Sejong was born near Kyongbok Palace in Hanyang, now called Seoul. Only two years earlier King T'aejo had moved the capital from Kaesong to Hanyang. King T'aejo had formed this new dynasty, which would last more than 500 years, only five years before. The dynastic succession of the early Yi Dynasty would change rather quickly. By 1399, Sejong's uncle Chongjong became king. Within a year, November 1400 by the lunar calendar, Chongjong abdicated in favor of Sejong's father Prince Chong-an, also known as Pangwon. When Pangwon ascended to the throne he took the name of T'aejong. So within three years of his birth Sejong became the son of the king of Korea. However, Sejong's oldest broth-

Portrait of the sage King Sejong

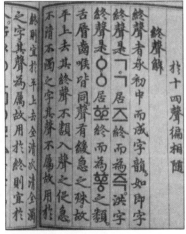

LEFT *Hunmin jongum*, the original explanation of the Korean alphabet devised by King Sejong   RIGHT Ancient rain guage developed during Sejong's reign

er was next in line to become king. Young Sejong was apparently not concerned much with becoming king. From the earliest age Sejong was interested in learning and mostly reading books. Sejong married at an early age. At the age of twelve he married a young girl two years older than himself. King T'aejong watched young Sejong grow in wisdom as he continued his studies. By the time Sejong was twenty-two King T'aejong decided to make him Crown Prince and successor to the throne over his older brother. Soon afterward his father decided to turn over the throne to his son. Many in the king's court protested, including Sejong, that the lad was not yet ready to shoulder such responsibility. King T'aejong insisted however and in 1419 Sejong became king.

King Sejong had a philosophy that the basis for good government depended on a king who could recognize and train men of good talent and utilize them in administering the various branches of his government. With that in mind King Sejong established the Jade Hall of Scholars (Chip'yonjon) which was a combination of the previous Hall of Art and the Hall of Literature and included a large library. King Sejong then selected twenty of his many able scholars and made them masters of learning allowing them to devote their full time to advanced learning. He also sought out hidden talent in the countryside by setting up a system that provided for individuals who distinguished themselves to be recognized by the provincial governor and reported to the king. These individuals often then had the chance to be appointed as government officials or given other posts according to their abilities.

One of King Sejong's goals, and the one for which he is most famous, was to make his people more educated by making it easier for them to become literate. At that time Koreans used the Chinese system of writing to document their spoken language. Chinese writing consists of thousands of individual characters that take significant effort to master. King Sejong put his efforts into developing a writing system that was simple and effective. By 1443 he had completed the Hangul alphabet. King Sejong was so concerned with its perfection that he kept it for another three years testing and modifying it to his satisfaction. This phonetic writing system was originally 28 letters consisting of 11 vowels and 17 consonants but has since been reduced to 24 letters consisting of 10 vowels and 14 consonants. The system was given to the people in 1446. Initially, there was much resistance to it from scholars who thought it would, among other things, limit the scholarly study of the Chinese classics. The king insisted however, and ordered many of his scholars to begin translating classic books and Buddhist scriptures into *han-gul*. This greatly increased the ability of the common person to become educated. In addition, he ordered books written to help the common man such as the *Farmers Handbook*, which provided guidance on farming methods and techniques to increase production. He directed other more technical books be written such as a complete medical dictionary and a pharmaceutical encyclopedia which contained 85 volumes of medical therapies, acupuncture techniques and herbal prescriptions treating 959 diseases. King Sejong promoted art, music, astronomy, science and inventions also. He is credited with development of the rain gauge and movable type print to name just a few.

    King Sejong had some impressive political achievements also. During his reign he was able to subjugate the Japanese pirates who had been raiding the Korean coast for many years. He also extended the territory of Korea north to the Yalu River. Domestically, he tried to control graft and corruption and raise the moral standards of the entire country.

    At last however, King Sejong was afflicted with a paralysis which prevented him from speaking more than a few words at a time. He later developed a cancer and died at the age of 52. His tomb is located in Yoju. His thirty-two year reign was studded with impressive social, political, academic and scientific achievement. It was a kind of golden period for Korea of which Koreans are very proud.

    Today, in downtown Seoul, the main thoroughfare running north to south in front of Kyongbok Palace bears his name. In addition two holidays are related to him; Han-gul day (9 October) and King Sejong Day (15 May). The King Sejong Memorial Society in northeastern Seoul boasts a museum and library relating to him and the study of *han-gul*.

12
First Female Ruler of Korea

Queen Sondok
(?- 647)

The first woman ever to ascend a throne in Korea, Queen Sondok was a kind and respected ruler. Her fifteen year reign as Queen of the Shilla Kingdom (632-647) experienced both peace and war during Korea's Three Kingdoms period. She is noted for her wisdom and foresight and there are many stories and legends about her great predictive powers.

The Korean peninsula was a violent place in the early seventh century. The nothern kingdom of Koguryo, under the leadership of General Ulchi Mundok, smashed the forces of Sui Dynasty China in 612 and the Sui Dynasty soon gave way to the Tang Dynasty in 618. The southwestern kingdom of Paekche and the southeastern kingdom of Shilla had long been struggling with Koguryo for supremacy of the peninsula. Territory was often lost, recaptured and lost again and borders changed frequently during this period with all three straining to gain advantage. Shilla King Chinpyung had reigned for more than fifty years when he finally died in 632. He failed to leave any male heirs to his throne and his eldest daughter, Tok-man (Sondok is her posthumous title), stepped forward to rule. Prior to Sondok's reign all Shilla

Ch'omsongdae, the famous astronomical observatory in Kyongju, which was built during Queen Sondok's reign

LEFT *Samguk Yusa (Story of the Three Kingdoms)* which includes some examples of Queen Sondok's predictive powers   RIGHT Tomb of Queen Sondok in Kyongju

monarchs had been members of the Pak clan. Sondok, however, broke this line as she was a member of the Kim clan which began its rise to prominence from that time forward.

Many cultural and religious advancements were noted during her short reign. Son, or Zen, Buddhism was said to have been introduced to Korea during Sondok's rule although it did not become popular until almost two hundred years later. Also during her reign, in 634, the great stone astronomical observatory, Ch'omsongdae, was built and is considered the oldest such observatory in Asia. It still stands today as National Treasure Number 31, and is considered one of the most important historical structures in Korea. Another famous structure ordered built by the queen was the famous wooden pagoda at Hwangnyongsa Temple near Kyongju. This nine story pagoda was built to protect Shilla from evil after the famous Shilla Buddhist monk, Chajang had a dream that the dragon spirit was protecting Shilla from her neighbors and a temple should be built to honor the spirit. When he reported his dream to Sondok, she ordered the temple built, the nine stories representing the nine neighbors the dragon spirit was protecting the kingdom from. Unfortunately, the temple was destroyed during the Mongol invasions of the thirteenth century but enough of the foundation remains to provide a detailed picture of what it was like. A great number of other temples and pagodas were built during her reign, many of which still stand today.

Sondok is most famous for her predictive powers and there are many stories celebrating her abilities. One such story is told in the *Samguk Yusa* as one of the three great prophecies of the queen. One cold winter day in 636 a large number of frogs were heard croaking at the Okmun pond. It was not natural for these frogs to be croaking, in the cold weather, and they had been doing so for a few days. When the queen saw the frogs she immediately knew they were warning her of an impending attack against her kingdom by Paekche forces. Although her generals had received no warning of military troops advancing she ordered two of her best generals, Alch'on and P'ilt'an, to pick two thousand of their best troops and march into Womans Valley, west of Kyongju, and destroy the enemy they would find there. The two Shilla generals dutifully set out, with a thousand troops each, and upon arriving in the valley found five hundred Paekche forces camped there. The Shilla forces surrounded and annihilated them including their commanding general, Usu. Later, they intercepted another Paekche force of over a thousand men, on its way to invade Shilla, and killed and or dispersed this entire force. Thus Sondok's foresight had saved the kingdom from surprise attack.

Another famous prophecy of Sondok's was the exact prediction of her death. She had told her attendants the exact day, month and year of her expected death and although no one believed her at the time, it too came true as she said.

Toward the end of her reign, each of the Three Kingdoms were attempting good relations with Tang Dynasty China in order to gain advantage over the other. Sondok was successful in winning the favor of China who helped her negotiate a temporary peace with Koguryo. The Paekche kingdom, however, under King Uija, was intent on destroying Shilla and fighting between the two kingdoms continued almost three more decades.

In the last years of her reign, Sondok, served by able and famous generals such as, Kim Yu-shin, was able to suppress a rebellion by a minority who wanted to gain power for themselves. Shortly after the rebellion, she died as predicted, and was succeeded by her sister, (or cousin, sources differ), Chindok. Shilla continued to grow stronger after her death, and eventually absorbed both Paekche and Koguryo, finally unifying the peninsula in 668.

Sondok was buried, as she requested, on the slopes of Namsan mountain near Kyongju. Her tomb, the stone observatory, and many other structures built by her orders can be visited today.

13
Founder of the Koryo Dynasty

Wang Kon
(877 - 943)

The founder and first king of the Koryo Dynasty, Wang Kon was a brilliant military general before he was unexpectedly thrust onto the throne. Through his short reign he achieved some impressive accomplishments. The entire southern part of the peninsula was again unified by Wang Kon and he was able to organize the beginnings of a central government. The rest of his dynasty, which was to last over 475 years, would produce many significant cultural and economic gains. Koryo would become famous for its celadon pottery and the country was an active trader with many other countries and even Arab ships would call at its ports. All of this began with the exploits of one man who was, at once, a soldier and a diplomat.

Not much is written about the early life of Wang Kon but it is believed he came from a wealthy family in the town of Kaegyong, now called Kaesong, in present day North Korea. His family apparently became rich from the lucrative trade with China in that period. The Korea of his youth, in the late ninth century, was in turmoil. The Shilla Dynasty, which had unified the southern part of the peninsula in 668,

Wang Kon's tomb in Kaesong, North Korea

The Koryo Dynasty Wang Kon founded became prosperous and noted for its beautiful celadon pottery *(Koryo Ch'ongja)* and rich Buddhist culture

had begun to crumble. Various rebellions erupted in the kingdom and one rebel leader, Kyonhwon, became strong enough in 892, to form the Kingdom of Later Paekche in the southwestern portion of the peninsula. Kungye, the son of another rebel leader, joined forces with Wang Kon, who was a rebel leader in his own area. They formed the Kingdom of Later Koguryo, in 901, in the center portion of the peninsula, with its capital at the city of Ch'orwon and with Kungye as its leader. This period became known as the Later Three Kingdoms period.

Due to some striking naval maneuvers and other successful military tactics against the Later Paekche Kingdom, Wang Kon became a respected leader. Kungye recognized his ability and made him the chief minister in his new government but Kungye allegedly developed into an abusive leader and, in 918, Wang Kon, backed by the other generals in the kingdom, overthrew him and established his own dynasty with the capital at Kaesong.

His task was only one third finished, however. The new Koryo Dynasty still had to contend with the Shilla and Later Paekche Kingdoms. Shilla was the weaker of the two and Koryo and Later Paekche constantly battled over its spoils. Both Koryo and Later Paekche maintained relations with China, Koryo mostly with northern China and Later Paekche mostly with the south. China was not much help to either Wang Kon or Kyonhwon's Later Paekche as China was itself experiencing internal disarray in a period known as the Five Dynasties.

Ultimately, Wang Kon persisted and Later Paekche began to weaken. With victories at Koch'ong in 930 and Unju in 934 Later Paekche was on the verge of defeat. By 935, Wang Kon finally defeated Later Paekche and in 936 King Kyongsun, of Shilla, also formally surrendered.

From the beginning, Wang Kon showed his diplomatic acumen by treating his conquered subjects with compassion and compromise. To the former Shilla King he gave a high government position and large landholdings in the Kyongju area which included a number of peasants to work the fields.

Wang Kon married a woman from the Shilla royal clan and gave other land grants to Shilla and Later Paekche officials who pledged their loyalty to him.

Although generous, Wang Kon was not foolish. To keep local leaders in tow he required certain sons of the local leaders to live in the capital as a kind of insurance to their allegiance and continued obedience. In addition, he established Buddhism as the state religion and decreed that while temples should be allowed autonomy there would be limits to their power and influence. He granted freedom to many slaves and a three year tax exemption to farmers to win their support.

After his initial consolidation, Wang Kon began to seek expansion. By 938, he incorporated Cheju Island into the kingdom and enlarged the territory to the north towards the Yalu River. Many military forts were constructed and other public works projects were begun. Many other projects and programs initiated by Wang Kon took generations to complete. Unfortunately, he did not live long enough to securely establish his system of government but he had the foresight to leave his successors his list of Ten Rules, to guide the nation. His many marriages, originally intended to insure loyalty ironically created many possible successors. When he died, in 943, power struggles immediately began.

Although the Koryo Dynasty he established had difficulties after his death it did prosper and survive for many generations. As was the custom, sometime after his death he was given the title, T'aejo, meaning Great Progenitor. Wang Kon was an able military tactician and an effective political leader. He was able to capitalize on the circumstances of his time and fashion prosperity from the ensuing turbulence.

14
Military Leader and Founder of the Yi Dynasty

Yi Song-gye
(King T'aejo, 1335–1408)

Before he became a king he was an able Koryo Dynasty general. He fought many successful battles for other rulers until he decided to rule himself. T'aejo, as he is more commonly called, founded the most recent and final dynasty of Korea. His dynasty, known as the Yi Dynasty (or Choson Dynasty), would last over five hundred years, the longest of the unified dynasties. His most noted accomplishments include moving the capital city from Kaesong to Seoul and transforming Korea into a distinctively Confucian state.

T'aejo was born in the late Koryo Dynasty to a family of military leaders who had distinguished themselves in battles against the dreaded Mongols years before. T'aejo had accompanied his father, Yi Whan-jo, a military general and prefect in Hamgyong Province, on many of his expeditions and undoubtedly gained valuable experience in the making. By 1361, T'aejo's father was appointed general over all the Koryo forces in the northeast part of the peninsula. When his father died in that position sometime later, T'aejo was allowed to take his place. T'aejo became a military man and quickly rose up through the Koryo army by impressive vic-

ABOVE This monument commemorates Yi Song-gye's victory over Japanese pirates before he founded the Choson Dynasty
LEFT Portrait of T'aejo Yi Song-gye

Kunjongjon in Kyongbok Palace built in the third year of Yi Song-gye's reign

tories against various enemies of the state.

His first task was to suppress a rebellion, within his own province, which he did without much effort. As a result he was promoted to military governor of the northeast and assigned the permanent command of the troops there. T'aejo was not much older than twenty-six at the time. Soon a far greater task would challenge his ability. The Red Turbans, an army of Chinese renegades, attacked across the Yalu River, in the northwest, and quickly advanced to the Koryo capital of present day Kaesong, forcing the king to flee south. When it seemed no one could halt their advance T'aejo attacked and captured the Red Turban leader and effected a smashing victory against their band. Koryo continued to be infected with incursions from the north and raids in the south by Japanese pirates. T'aejo was called upon time and again to save the country and frequently delivered spectacular victories, especially against the Mongols in the mid 1360's.

T'aejo was not the only great commander of the period. Koryo was blessed with at least two such renowned leaders, the other being general Ch'oe Yong. Ch'oe was the senior commander of the two and reportedly much loved among the Korean people. He was in frequent disagreement with his deputy, T'aejo, concerning national policy and the direction of military forces. Their disagreements later came to a head over how to deal with the Ming Dynasty China decision to virtually annex the northeastern portion of Korea. Ming China had driven out the Mongol Yüan Dynasty, in 1368, after nearly a century of rule. Initially, relations between Koryo and the new dynasty were cordial. The Koryo king sent a delegation to perform the required ceremonies and reaffirm the relationship as vassal. The Ming emperor responded in kind by releasing all the Koryo citizens who had been held by the Yüan Dynasty Mongols as hostages. He later sent Ming clothing which the Koryo Kingdom adopted and Koreans still model today even though a later Chinese dynasty changed their style of clothing to fit the style of their Manchu conquerors. The relations continued well while the Ming continued to establish itself and Koryo dealt with the ever present Japanese pirates and the still lingering threat from pockets of Mongol forces. T'aejo was a key commander during many expeditions to quell rebellions and keep order in the kingdom during this period.

In 1374, Koryo King Kongmin was assassinated and replaced by King Shinu. The Ming did not immediately recognize his reign but the Mongols quickly did, hoping to gain the support of Koryo against the Ming. In 1388, the Ming occupied key fortresses in Korea's northern region. The king and General Ch'oe ordered T'aejo to take strong forces and attack the Ming. He thought this unwise and resisted because he did not believe the smaller kingdom of Koryo could succeed against the much larger China. T'aejo began the expedition but met heavy rains which proved a formiddable obstacle. He finally decided to turn his forces around and attack his own capital instead of the Ming. He returned to Kaesong and ousted the king and General Ch'oe and began to install his own reform government. Over the next few years T'aejo continued a purge of the government and instituted a number of reforms including an important land reform. He reorganized the military by 1391, and had himself elevated to commander of all the forces. The following year, T'aejo proclaimed the start of a new dynasty. He soon sent a delegation to the Ming to gain their recognition and help choose a proper name for the dynasty. He proposed two choices, Choson, or Hwaryong which was the name of T'aejo's birthplace. The Chinese emperor chose Choson, which roughly translated means, morning calm, which in-turn, is how Korea became known as the Land of the Morning Calm. Within a few years, by 1395, T'aejo attempted to destroy any affiliation with old Koryo by moving the capital to a new location, Hanyang, or present day Seoul.

In the last few years of his reign there was much intrigue over which of his six sons would succeed him. T'aejo finally abdicated in 1398 and was succeeded by his son Yi Kyong, who became King Chongjong. The dynasty he created would enjoy many great accomplishments including the development of the Korean alphabet, and many great advances in science and the arts before it finally ended in 1910. T'aejo was the man who had the courage and foresight to turn the misfortune of one crumbling dynasty into the foundation of a new and stronger one.

III

MILITARY

Ch'oe Yong

Kang Kam-ch'an

Kim Yu-shin

Kyebaek

Ulchi Mundok

Yi Sun-shin

15
Respected Koryo General

Ch'oe Yong
(1316-1389)

One of the many famous generals of the Koryo Dynasty, Ch'oe was an able leader and was well liked by the people. He successfully repelled repeated attacks by Japanese pirates and led expeditions into China to help quell rebellion. Through his efforts many northern territories were returned to Korean control. His fierce loyalty to the declining Koryo Dynasty would ultimately cost him his head when the Yi Dynasty, under the leadership of his former subordinate, Yi Song-gye, displaced the Koryo Dynasty at the end of the fourteenth century.

Hailing from Ch'orwon in Kangwon Province, Ham Sok-hon describes him in his book *Queen of Suffering,* as fierce in appearance, with unusual physical strength, firm of will, upright and pure of heart. His beginnings were humble and his lifestyle can be best described as spartan. He gave little notice to his own clothes and meals and eschewed fine garments or other comforts, even when he became famous and could have easily enjoyed them. He disliked men who relished expensive articles and he viewed simplicity as a virtue. Such a man was well suited for military service and

Portrait of Ch'oe Yong, respected Koryo general

Ch'oe quickly gained the confidence of his men and his king during numerous battles with Japanese pirates who began seriously raiding the Korean coast around 1350.

At thirty-six years old he became a national hero when he successfully put down a rebellion by Cho Il-shin who had surrounded the palace, killed many officials, and proclaimed himself premier. Just a few years later, in 1355, a rebellion erupted in Yüan Dynasty China, which was already experiencing great internal turmoil itself. Ch'oe was sent to help the Mongols quell that rebellion and his success in twenty-seven battles helped him win even more favor and fame at home. Upon returning to Korea, he dutifully reported the internal problems of the dying Yüan Dynasty which gave Koryo King Kongmin the notion that the time was ripe to recover some of the northern territories previously lost to the Mongols. Again, Ch'oe fought to recover various towns west of the Yalu River to the delight of the king. For the next few years, Ch'oe turned his attention to the marauding Japanese pirates who he battled continuously. He served a brief stint as the Mayor of Pyongyang where his efforts at increasing crop production and decreasing hunger won him even more attention as a national hero. Ch'oe continued to distinguish himself when in 1363, a high government official named Kim Yong-an tried to take control of the government and Ch'oe was forced to battle a 10,000 man Mongol force which attacked Koryo in conjunction with the rebellion. Just a year after he defeated the Mongol force, fate took a strange turn for Ch'oe, which almost completely ruined his life.

King Kongmin had a terrible dream, one night in 1365, that someone would try to stab him and a Buddhist monk would intervene to save his life. The king awoke relieved but could not forget the face of the monk. Astonishingly he met a monk, Shin Ton, sometime later, that looked like the monk in his dream. The king promoted the monk to high position and allowed him considerable influence. Shin Ton was ruthless and corrupt, however, and Ch'oe who relentlessly exposed corruption in the kingdom, became at odds with him. Shin Ton engineered accusations of misconduct against Ch'oe that brought the great general a punishment of six years in exile and brought him uncomfortably close to the death penalty. When Shin Ton died, Ch'oe was restored to his position and asked to prepare a fleet to fight the Japanese pirates and eliminate the remaining Mongol forces on Cheju Island. He first engaged the Mongols, who fought tenaciously, but Ch'oe's forces eventually freed the island. Ch'oe continued to fight the Japanese pirates who would unfortunately remain a menace, long after Ch'oe's death, to the end of the century. In 1375, King Kongmin died and was replaced by King Shinu who many believe was actually a son of the monk Shin Ton.

Another great general, Yi Song-gye, was rising through the ranks during this period. Like Ch'oe, Yi's relentless warring with the Japanese pirates, especially during the late 1370's and early 1380's, also brought him great fame and favor. Ch'oe remained the senior officer throughout both their careers but he and Yi were in frequent disagreement over the direction of national policy and the use of military force (see chapter 14). There disagreements finally came to a head over how to deal with Ming Dynasty China's move into Koryo's northern territories.

Ming China had risen out of the old Mongol Yüan Dynasty in 1368. The Mongols were basically down but not out, and for some time Koryo Korea vacillated between the two forces taking advantage where they could siding with one then the other. When the Ming encroached on Koryo's northern territories however, King Shinu ordered an expedition in 1388, to drive them out. At seventy-two years of age Ch'oe was made commander-in-chief, but the younger Yi was put in command of the actual force. Yi argued against the plan claiming it was suicidal to attack the much stronger Ming forces and to attempt it in the worst season for military operations. The king would tolerate no disagreement, however, and Yi initially set out with his forces but, after encountering heavy rains, made the daring decision to turn around and take control of his own country instead of warring with the Chinese. When Yi returned Ch'oe put up a gallant fight at the palace but was overwhelmed. Records differ as to what happened next, some say Ch'oe was banished to Koyang and others say he was later beheaded, it is likely that both are true.

Regardless of his fate, Ch'oe is remembered as a great Koryo general who was devoted to the protection of his country. His ultimate loyalty cost him his life but he had bravely risked his life many times before in the defense of his country.

16
Courageous Koryo Military Leader

Kang Kam-ch'an
(948 –1031)

One of the great military commanders of Korea, Kang's military genius was renowned during the early Koryo Dynasty. With his help Koryo was able to successfully repel the many invasions of its northern border and his efforts in particular battles saved the very existence of the dynasty. He is remembered as an able general with fierce courage and strong loyalty to both his men and his country.

Kang was born in southern Seoul, near Kwanak Mountain, in what is now Pongch'on-dong. The legend has it that a huge star fell on the night of his birth which made all who knew believe this lad was surely destined for greatness. He would, in time, fulfill this legend with many military accomplishments that propelled him into the history books as a national hero.

Early Koryo Korea after the death of the founder, Wang Kon in 943, experienced leadership difficulties. Although Kang was born only five years after the Koryo founder's death, Koryo was already into the reign of its third king, Chongjong (Wang Yo), and Kang's life would span the reign of six kings. The kingdom shared northern borders, with the

ABOVE **Portrait of Kang Kam-Ch'an** LEFT **A representation of Kang's many battles with the Khitan forces**

Statue of Kang mounted for battle, located at P'altal Park in Suwon, and stele of Kang at Naksongdae in Seoul

Jurchens to the northeast and the Khitans to the northwest. These two neighbors, the Khitans in particular, were a constant annoyance to Koryo and their frequent incursions into Koryo territory created serious cause for concern. To the west, China itself was undergoing dynastic changes and the normal turmoil that results from the subsequent consolidation period. The Sung Dynasty in China had formed the year before Kang's birth and the Khitans had established their state of Liao in Manchuria the same year. Kang grew up during the period of their growth with which Koryo became inextricably entangled.

Ironically, Kang advanced in civilian, not military, government positions. He had scored high in the government service exams and had received some recognition for his wisdom and intelligence. By the late tenth century, the Sung Dynasty was extending its influence northward and the Khitans had expanded themselves east to the Yalu River. The Khitans pursued an alliance with Koryo against the Sung but Koryo was not favorably inclined. In October 993, the Khitans swooped down from the north with over 800,000 men advancing deep into Korea. They demanded Koryo cease their relations with the Sung and become a vassal of the Khitans. A negotiated peace in which Koryo yielded to some demands suspended further attacks and temporarily improved relations between the two countries.

In the early eleventh century, the seventh ruler of Koryo, King Mokchong, was assassinated (1009). Under the guise of "helping to punish" those responsible, the Khitans attacked Koryo with over 400,000 troops. Their advance was only temporarily slowed and they eventually seized the capital of Kaegyong and forced the king and his court to flee south to the Cholla Province city of Naju. The Khitans again demanded the subservience of Koryo. Kang advised the king to bide his time and slowly wear down the invaders. The tactic was successful and constant harassment by Koryo forces contributed to an eventual withdrawal of the Khitans back across the Yalu. Afterward, Kang was given the close confidence of the king and his advice was respected even more at court.

The next few years produced many more Khitan attacks which were usually suspended during the harsh winters only to be renewed the following spring. During this time Koryo made several appeals for Sung assistance against the Khitans but the Sung showed little interest at that time. Koryo was forced to settle the problem on their own and by 1018 they were better prepared to face the Khitans. The Koryo army was improved and placed under the command of Kang, and when the Khitans launched their third major invasion that year, Kang was prepared.

Kang had constructed a dam in a strategic valley and a considerable lake had amassed behind it. He lured the Khitans into the valley, and at the right time he destroyed the dam sweeping many of the soldiers away in the deluge. Kang's troops fell upon the remaining panic stricken Khitan's and annihilated them. Later he scored two more quick victories for the Koryo army driving the invaders back to their home. The following year, the Khitans attacked again, but Kang was again prepared, he defeated their forces at Yongbyon and caused their retreat to Kwiju where they made their final stand. The Khitans fought fiercely but Kang would not let up and ultimately destroyed all but a few thousand of their army which escaped back across the Yalu River.

When Kang returned with the news, along with many Khitan heads and captured supplies, he was given a hero's welcome. King Hyonjong personally met him and presented him eight golden flowers. Kang retired the following year and received a huge estate and six honorary titles. He was known as the "Pillar of Koryo" until his death some years later. The Khitans continued to exist as a nation for almost a century but never again did they attempt to raid Korea as before.

Naksongdae, Kang's birthplace, is a very pleasant park and memorial to him. It is located in Pongch'on-dong nestled in the mountains of southern Seoul. A few hundred meters away, and a bit more difficult to find, is the actual spot where Kang was born. A small stele marks this small patch of land but apartments have been built up around it which makes it difficult to locate. Just south of Seoul about two hours' drive, is Kang's tomb. It is located in North Ch'ungch'ong Province, in Oksan-myon.

17
Revered Military Leader of the Shilla Dynasty

Kim Yu-shin
(595 – 673)

Certainly, the greatest general produced by the Shilla Dynasty, Kim may well be the most famous Korean general of all time. His extraordinary leadership during major battles, at the end of the Three Kingdoms period, led to key victories which allowed the Shilla Kingdom to unite the peninsula. He is the focus of many stories and legends and is familiar to most Koreans from a very early age.

The Korean peninsula of the late sixth century was comprised of three major kingdoms; Koguryo to the north, Paekche to the southwest and Shilla to the southeast. These three kingdoms each produced many great leaders and had significant accomplishments but they were constant rivals. Their great neighbor to the west, China, was at that time, governed under the Sui Dynasty, which had united that country in 589. Shilla had arranged an alliance with Sui to attempt to counterbalance the power of the larger kingdom of Koguryo. Three years after Kim Yu-shin was born, in 598, Koguryo attacked Sui and acquired some key defensive positions in China. Sui counterattacked but was beaten back. Some years later, in 612, Sui prepared a more powerful force

Portrait of the famous general Kim Yu-shin and statue of Kim leading the charge into battle

but this time they were more severely beaten by Koguryo forces. This defeat proved disastrous for Sui and they were replaced by the Tang Dynasty in 618.

It was in this context, of strong warring neighbors, that Kim became a man. In this period of constant power struggles between the Three Kingdoms and China Kim grew up and became enthralled with the military arts. He is reported to have been a master swordsman by the age of eighteen, and had already become a Hwarang some three years before. The Hwarang was a kind of patriotic youth corps developed in Shilla. Its members were young men of noble birth who chose the art of warfare as a way of contributing to their kingdom. In some ways, the Hwarang was a primitive West Point in that it provided essential military training and discipline to these future leaders of Shilla. The Hwarang produced many such leaders who later helped Shilla unite and govern the Korean peninsula.

It was during this impressionable age, as a Hwarang, that he fell in love with a famous entertainer named Ch'ung-wan. This encounter became the basis for a famous love story that is still popular today. The story ended tragically and Kim went off to Chiri Mountain to continue his training in seclusion for some seven years.

His first military appointment is believed to have occurred around 629 and he quickly proved his value as a capable warrior. Shilla was in a constant struggle with its neighbor to the west, Paekche, over territory. There had been gains on both sides and the struggle lasted for many years. It was during this period that Kim rose through the ranks of the military. It was as a commander in the field, that he was to make his mark.

Shilla sought the aid of Tang Dynasty China to counter the combined forces of Paekche and Koguryo. Tang, who had suffered many defeats against the powerful Koguryo forces, was anxious to recoup their previous losses. When Koguryo and Paekche attacked Shilla, in 655, Shilla joined forces with Tang to battle the invaders. Although it is not clear when Kim first became a general, he was commanding the Shilla forces at this time. Eventually with the help of the Shilla navy, which had grown to considerable strength, and some 13,000 Tang forces, Kim attacked the Paekche capital, Puyo, in 660. This resulted in one of the most famous battles of the century. The Paekche defenders were commanded by none other than, Kyebaek, another distinguished general. In the end, Paekche forces, numbering only about 5,000, were no match for Kim's warriors, which numbered about ten times as many. Paekche, who had been experiencing internal political problems, crumbled. Kim's Shilla forces and the armies of the Tang now turned to face Koguryo from two directions. By 661 they attacked the seemingly impregnable Koguryo Kingdom and again were driven back. Koguryo was staggering however, and in 667 another offensive was launched which, finally in 668, broke the back of Koguryo forever. Shilla still had to subdue various pockets of resistance but their next effort was to ensure their Chinese allies did not overstay their welcome on the peninsula. With some effort, Shilla forced out the Tang and united the peninsula under their rule.

Kim had been handsomely rewarded for his efforts. He reportedly received a village of over 500 households. In addition, he was reportedly given some 142 separate horse farms throughout the kingdom in 669. Kim died some four years later at the age of seventy-eight. He had one brother and two younger sisters. He left behind ten children two of whom became famous in their own right. His first son Munmu, rose to be the 30th king of the Shilla Dynasty. His second, and reportedly favorite son, Won-sul, also became a famous general.

Kim was buried in Kyongju, on the southeast coast of Korea. His splendid tomb is National Historic Site #21 and is popular among visitors to Kyongju. Kim's loyalty and ability are legendary and have survived more than thirteen centuries to make him one of the oldest heroes of Korea.

18
The Pride of Paekche

Kyebaek
(? - 660)

Probably the most well-known military leader from the Paekche Kingdom during the Three Kingdoms period, he is also one of the leading historical military characters of Korea. Although his military success was notable it was small in comparison to other great Korean leaders. Kyebaek is most famous for his personal characteristics and virtue. He personified many of the personal qualities Koreans, and indeed people all over the world, regard highly. So even in military defeat he is remembered for his loyalty, dedication, self sacrifice for his nation, leadership and forgiveness of his enemies.

In the context of northeast Asia of the seventh century, the Korean peninsula as well as activities on the mainland of China were relatively unstable. Korea was in the last stages of its Three Kingdoms period with the powerful Koguryo Kingdom occupying the northern part of the peninsula, Paekche to the southwest, and the Shilla to the southeast. The Paekche was the weaker of the three during the seventh century, with the once powerful Koguryo slowly losing its stature and the rising Shilla Kingdom gaining momentum that would ultimately allow it to unite the peninsula under

Portrait of Kyebaek, man of honor and military hero of the Paekche Kingdom   BELOW Statue of Kyebaek watching over his troops

its rule in the later part of that century. The mighty neighbor to the west, China, had itself only relatively recently been united in the late sixth century under the Sui Dynasty. That dynasty had its own problems including those with the then powerful Koguryo Kingdom of northern Korea, and after some disastrous defeats at the hands of Koguryo forces under the leadership of General Ulchi Mundok (see chapter 19) the Sui Dynasty was replaced by the Tang Dynasty in 618. The Tang Dynasty would assist in shaping the power balance on the Korean peninsula by allying with Paekche's rival, Shilla Kingdom, in a war that would propell Kyebaek into fame and honor.

Relatively little is written about Kyebaek's early life and very little detail, including his birthdate and birthplace, is known about him. We do know when he died however, and from that we can safely assume that he grew up in the Paekche Kingdom during these political changes both on the peninsula and in China. We also know that Kyebaek was fiercely loyal to the kingdom and its king even though the last years of Paekche had seen a disastrous decay in its strength largely due to a king who ignored his kingdom in favor or pursuing his personal pleasures.

The Paekche of Kyebaek's adulthood was ruled by King Uija (641-660) who initially appeared as a strong and able ruler. In 642 he launched some military expeditions against Shilla taking some key fortifications on its northern border. Again in 655, he initiated another offensive that engulfed some thirty Shilla fortresses. After these successes however, he lapsed into disinterest and ignored the counteroffensive that was building against him.

In March 660, Shilla alligned with Tang Dynasty China to attack the Paekche Kingdom with the hope of conquering it then closing the grip on the Koguryo Kingdom to the north. The Tang Emperor, Kao-tsung sent approximately 130,000 troops in 1,900 ships to attack Paekche from the west. Simultaneously, 50,000 Shilla forces under the leadership of the famous general Kim Yu-shin (see chapter 17), set out to attack Paekche from the east. Kyebaek took 5,000 of his best troops and marched out to meet the Shilla forces. He knew his efforts were futile before he set out, and he reportedly stated "I would rather die than be a slave of the enemy." Kyebaek then killed his wife and family rather than allow them to fall into the hands of opposing forces, or allow the thought of them to influence his actions, or cause him to falter in battle. Initially, Kyebaek had some success against Shilla winning four small battles. In one of the battles, Shilla General P'ummok sent his sixteen year old son, Kwanch'ang, to fight at the front. Kyebaek captured Kwanch'ang but was moved because of his great courage. Kyebaek released the young warrior only to meet and capture him again in another battle.

Kyebaek later moved his forces to block the advance of General Kim Yu-shin. They met on the plains of Hwangsan Field, in present day Hamyang, near Chiri Mountain. Kyebaek's forces fought bravely but they were outnumbered ten to one. In the end, Kyebaek and his men were completely defeated. The Shilla forces went on to overcome all of Paekche and then, with the help of Tang forces defeated Koguryo forces and united the entire peninsula in 668.

Kyebaek suffered a great defeat without humility. He set out to defend his country with meager forces, badly outnumbered, confident he would surely die. This did not cause him to hesitate, in fact, he sacrificed his whole family in addition to himself for the sake of his country. He did this even though his king and country had decayed to a point where many did not believe either deserved such devotion. In the midst of battle and in such despair, he still possessed the compassion to recognize courage in the enemy and spare the young boy Kwanch'ang. All these honorable attributes Kyebaek exemplified to the very end. He is remembered as a man of honor and national hero of Korea.

19
Koguryo's Fearless General
Ulchi Mundok
(? - ?)

Probably the most distinguished military leader of the Koguryo period and one of the most well-known generals in Korean history, General Ulchi Mundok's leadership and tactical knowledge was the decisive factor in saving Koguryo Korea from destruction at the hands of Chinese forces of the Sui Dynasty. He faced invading forces of far superior numbers and not only turned them back but was able to pursue and destroy them with such vigor that they were not able nor inclined to return. Much of his early life's story is sketchy but his later life was filled with enough spectacular success to earn him a permanent place among Korea's most remembered.

It is not known when this great man was born or in exactly what place and unfortunately it is not known exactly when he died. Even based on records of his accomplishments the best that can be said is that he was born in the mid sixth century and died in the early seventh century sometime after 618. It is certain that he was born and raised in a turbulent era both on the Korean peninsula and in neighboring China. His life spanned the later portion of an era known

Portrait of the great hero of the Koguryo Kingdom, Ulchi Mundok

as the Three Kingdoms period of Korea. The Koguryo Kingdom to the north was Ulchi Mundok's home. It was a powerful and warlike kingdom, aggressive and strong enough to have lasted from 37 B.C. until 668. The two neighbors to the south, Shilla to the southeast and Paekche to the southwest, were bitter enemies and the three kingdoms constantly vied for each other's territory and ultimate power on the peninsula. The balance of power was somewhat equal during that period, however, and needed the infusion of outside forces to tip the scales in some direction. This force was supplied by their much larger western neighbor, China.

China itself was transforming in the late sixth century. For more than 350 years China had been composed of smaller kingdoms struggling for power, much like Korea, in an era known as the Six Dynasties period. In 589 however, China was united under the new Sui Dynasty. This new dynasty would supply the force needed to influence the balance of power on the Korean peninsula.

Ulchi Mundok grew up during this transformation in China and during the decline of the Koguryo Kingdom and the rise in power of the Shilla Kingdom on the Korean peninsula. He was an educated man, an eventual Minister of Koguryo, with skills in both the political and military sciences. He would be called upon to render service as a military leader, however, when the very existence of the kingdom became threatened by alliances between its rival neighbors.

Sui Dynasty China had a terrible suspicion of its warlike neighbor, Koguryo, and it did not enjoy good relations with the Sui as did Koguryo's rivals, Shilla and Paekche. Finally in 612, Yang Ti, the Sui Dynasty emperor, decided to subdue his dangerous neighbor and prepared to attack Koguryo. According to Chinese accounts, Emperor Yang Ti prepared a force of over one million men and personally led them against Koguryo. They quickly overran Koguryo outposts, camped on the Liao River and prepared to bridge the river. Ulchi Mundok was called upon to assist in the defense of the nation. He prepared to meet the superior Sui forces with a strategy of retreat, deception and attack. After the Sui forces crossed the Liao river a small contingent was sent to attack the city of Liaotung. General Ulchi Mundok sent his forces to meet them there and drove them out in a rout. The Sui forces tried other probes of little significance biding their time until the rainy season passed. Following the rainy season the Sui moved their forces to the banks of the Yalu River in northwestern Korea and prepared for a major assault. General Ulchi Mundok visited the Chinese camp under the guise of surrender in an attempt to discover any weakness of the force. The king listened to General Ulchi Mundok and allowed him to leave the camp. Shortly after, Emperor Yang Ti changed his mind and set out after the general but it was too late. The general had discovered what he needed to defeat the force. He learned that the Sui forces were short of provisions and had overstretched their supply lines. General Ulchi Mundok decided to pursue a strategy of gradual retreat, luring his enemy deeper into hostile territory. He fought a kind of guerrilla warfare, picking when and where he fought and allowing the Sui forces to feel as though victory was close at hand, while luring them deeper into his trap. An advance force of over 300,000 was sent to take the city of Pyongyang. General Ulchi Mundok continued to lure them closer to the city to a strategic point where he could strike. His forces attacked from all sides driving the Sui troops back in utter confusion. Koguryo forces continued the pursuit slaughtering them almost at will. It is said that only 2,700 troops successfully made it back to the main body of forces. Winter soon began to set in and the Sui forces, short on provisions, were forced to return home. Beginning the following spring a second and third attack met similar disaster. Internal rebellion in China forced the Sui to give up its desires on Koguryo. By 618, the relatively short lived Sui Dynasty was replaced by the Tang Dynasty. General Ulchi Mundok's strategy and leadership had saved Koguryo Korea from the Chinese. Unfortunately for Koguryo, the emerging Shilla Kingdom would unite the peninsula some fifty years later.

General Ulchi Mundok is still celebrated as a great Korean hero. A main street in downtown Seoul, Ulchi-ro, is named for him. His victories are remembered as a time when the smaller Korean kingdom was able to decisively defeat the vastly larger Chinese nation.

20
Most Respected Military Hero

Yi Sun-shin
(1545 –1598)

Admiral Yi is one of Korea's most famous military heroes. He is most noted for his invention and use of the Turtle Ship, an ironclad warship that resembled a turtle in design. He used this ship to defeat the Japanese naval force that invaded Korea from 1592 to 1598. He was a brilliant naval strategist believed, by many, to have had no peer. In addition to his many naval victories, Admiral Yi is revered as a patriot and a strong and honorable defender of Korea.

Admiral Yi was born in Seoul on 28 April (8 March by the lunar calendar), 1545. He was born of a common family but through hard work and great persistence grew to be a respected man. At the age of 21 he began to learn the military arts through self-study and hard work as an apprentice to various makers of weapons. At age 28, he took the national government examinations to be commissioned as a military officer. During the practical exam on horseback riding, Admiral Yi fell and, as a result, did not pass. He continued preparing for the next exams, which were given four years later, and passed them at the age of thirty-two. He was commissioned as a junior officer and transferred to a remote

LEFT Portrait of Yi Sun-shin, who invented and used the Turtle Ship to defeat the Japanese naval force that invaded Korea from 1592 to 1598   BOTTOM Yi supervising the construction of his famous Turtle Ship

assignment on the Tumen River on the northern border of Korea. He held various posts until 1591 when he was assigned as the commander of the Left Cholla Naval Station. This post would position him to achieve fame during the 1592 Japanese invasion under the direction of Toyotomi Hideyoshi. It was before this expected invasion that Admiral Yi set about to build the famous Turtle Ship.

The Turtle Ship (*Kobukson* in Korean) was an ironclad warship which appeared centuries before the Monitor appeared in the American Civil War. The ship had a covered deck which was armor plated and had many sharp spikes and spears protruding from it to prevent enemy boarding. On the sides were portholes through which cannons were fired. The ship itself was propelled by ten oars on each side. From the bow, a four foot dragon's head protruded. By burning a combination of sulphur and saltpeter, clouds of smoke were emitted through the dragon's head and created a mist which helped mask the ship. With this vessel Admiral Yi faced the vastly superior numbers of the Japanese fleet.

Historical accounts show the Japanese invasion had significant initial success. Then Admiral Yi was summoned to attack the invaders. He first made contact in May 1592 at Okp'o, off the southeast coast of Korea, where he quickly destroyed twenty-six of the thirty ships anchored there with few losses of his own. Subsequently, Admiral Yi had numerous successes, over the next five years through 1597, including victories at Hansan Island, Pusan and the Myongnyang Strait, near Chindo on the southwestern coast. The Japanese reportedly did not win a single battle against him in the entire war.

Admiral Yi died during the last battle at Noryang Strait, on 16 December (19 November by lunar calendar), 1598, when a stray bullet struck him in the armpit. This battle, however, spoiled the Japanese advance in Korea and eventually forced them to give up their plans for conquest of the peninsula for that time.

Memorials to Admiral Yi abound in Korea. One of the most often seen is a statue of Admiral Yi and his Turtle Ship in downtown Seoul at the intersection of Sejong-no and Chong-no in the center of the city. Also, in downtown Seoul, the famous street of Ch'ungmu-ro is named after him, Ch'ungmu, meaning "Lord of Loyalty and Chivalry," is an official honorary title given to him after his death. Outside the capital are many additional memorials to the Admiral. In Asan-gun, about 85 kilometers south of Seoul, the Hyonch'ungsa Shrine was built in 1706 and is a Mecca for those who honor the Admiral. It is an expansive parklike shrine which includes the Admiral's house, archery range and a museum with many relics including a smaller scale replica of the Turtle Ship. Just a little farther north lies the Admiral's grave on a small secluded side of a small mountain. On the southeastern coast is the pleasant city of Ch'ungmu, which is also named for Admiral Yi. Ch'ungmu is home to many restored buildings which were part of the Admiral's headquarters during that period. In Chinhae, a replica of the Turtle Ship floats in the bay and in Hansan Bay stands a lighthouse atop a replica of a Turtle Ship which is still a favorite tourist attraction.

Admiral Yi is probably the Korean military hero best known outside of Korea. His story is well published in English books and pamphlets. He is of course, very well known within Korea and his record of accomplishments is too long to do justice in this short introduction.

IV

PHILOSOPHERS

Wonhyo

Yi Hwang

Yi Yi

21
Buddhist Evangelist

Wonhyo
(617 – 686)

During the period of the Shilla Dynasty there was no Buddhist figure more highly esteemed than Wonhyo. He was a great teacher and proselytizer of Buddhism. Even though he was not educated in, nor in fact ever visited China, he was respected there as well as in his native Korea. Born in the Three Kingdoms period and living part of his life in the Unified Shilla period, Wonhyo influenced many young people through his lectures and writings.

Toward the later part of the Three Kingdoms period in Korea, and one year before the Tang Dynasty replaced the Sui in China, Wonhyo was born in a village in Kyongsang Province, southeastern Korea. Sol was his family name; Wonhyo, meaning Breaking Dawn, later became his Buddhist name. Records of his early life are not detailed but it is believed Wonhyo became acquainted with Buddhism at an early age.

Buddhism had been introduced to Korea in the fourth century but had not reached Shilla until after 528, almost ninety years before Wonhyo was born. Soon after it was legalized in Shilla it became popular and was even support-

LEFT Portrait of Wonhyo, Buddhist evangelist of Shilla Dynasty

RIGHT Wonhyo wrote many books at Punhwangsa Temple in Kyongju where he stayed late in his life. This stone tower is all that remains of the temple

ed by the government who invited priests to help teach and spread the religion. Soon Buddhist ceremonies were substituted for many of the old religious rituals. When Shilla later formed the "Hwarang" or young warriors, Buddhism provided the spiritual guidance for the group.

Wonhyo grew up as a wandering monk, talking with other monks and scholars, and learning as he traveled. Most monks at some point received their formal Buddhist learning in China but not Wonhyo. He tried to travel to China twice but failed to make it. On one trip he journeyed with his friend Uisang, another distinguished monk. They made it only as far as Liaotung, which at that time belonged to the Koguryo Kingdom. The two were suspected as spies and questioned for ten days but eventually returned home. Again they tried some years later. Legend says they were halted by a severe storm and forced to sleep in an old tomb. There Wonhyo had a vision which led him to discover the truths he had been searching for. Feeling no further need to travel on to China he returned to Shilla leaving Uisang to travel on alone. Uisang would return some nine years later much enriched by his studies in Tang Dynasty China. Wonhyo however, did not suffer from his decision to stay in Shilla Korea. He continued learning as he began, through self-study, and was somehow able to attain the rank of high priest.

As a writer of Buddhist materials he was one of the most prolific of his time. He reportedly scribed some 180 volumes of materials covering a wide range of topics. Unfortunately, only a relative few of his works remain. Much of Wonhyo's effort attempted to unify and synthesize the various Buddhist sects that had transplanted and prospered from China to Korea. The sects were introduced by the many Buddhist scholars who studied in China and returned to spread their particular form of the religion. One of the most popular sects, Hwaom, was introduced by Wonhyo's old friend, Uisang, upon his return from his lone journey to Tang China years before. Seeking to transcend the differences of the various sects, Wonhyo worked to identify similarities and encouraged others to focus their thoughts as such. The common people were his main target group. In his later years, he traveled the peninsula living and preaching to the common man. At some point he fell in love with a widowed princess of Yosok palace. From this affair he fathered a son, Sol Ch'ong, who grew to be one of the ten great sages of Korea.

Somewhat troubled by the fact that his relations with the princess caused him to break his vow of celibacy, Wonhyo reportedly abandoned his Buddhist garments and traveled the countryside in more ordinary clothes. He began using the pen name, Sosong Kosa, which means, Little Hermit. He traveled the country preaching what some call, Pure Land Buddhism. This form of Buddhism teaches that all men can be born again in paradise. This concept greatly appealed to the common people and it is said that ninety percent of Shilla Dynasty citizens accepted Buddhism, which if accurate, is a remarkable evangelical record. As previously stated, Wonhyo was respected in both China and Japan. His non-sectarian approach to Buddhism was somewhat common during the Shilla Dynasty. This approach is sometimes called all-inclusive Buddhism or Whole Buddhism. Because of his life dedication to this eclectic approach, and the fame he achieved through it, he is sometimes referred to as the father or founder of Whole Buddhism.

In the seventh year of King Shinmun (686), Wonhyo died. Legends about him abound in Korea. This great Buddhist scholar truly personified the form of Buddhism he so fervently taught for much of his life.

22
Unparalleled Scholar and Philosopher

Yi Hwang
(T'oegye, 1501-1570)

T'oegye is a noted Korean sage. He is most famous as a master of Neo-Confucian philosophy. His writings are world renowned and also contributed to the advancement of Neo-Confucian philosophy in Japan during the Tokugawa period. T'oegye is his chosen penname and it means "Receding Stream."

T'oegye was born in Ye-an, near Andong in South Kyongsang Province in the southeastern part of Korea in 1501. He was the youngest of eight brothers. He never had the chance to know his father who died when T'oegye was one year old. His mother and his father's brother raised him. It is said he began his study of philosophy at the early age of twelve. T'oegye continued studying until he entered the famous Songgungwan University in Seoul in 1523, which was the national university and provided many of the Yi Dynasty's best Confucian scholars. At the age of 21 he married and had two sons but the story of his immediate family is filled with tragedy. Six years after he married, and shortly after the birth of his second son, his wife died unexpectedly. T'oegye remarried at age thirty and his second wife died

Tosan Sowon, Yi Hwang's academy in Andong where he studied and lectured Confucianism. He is the most respected scholar of Yi Dynasty

when he reached forty-six years of age. Two years later his second son also passed away.

In spite of much personal misfortune, T'oegye passed the civil administration examinations at the age of thirty-four and held a few government posts during the reign of Kings Chungjong and Myongjong, the eleventh and thirteenth kings of the Yi Dynasty. When he was about forty-nine years old he was appointed the governor of Tanyang. Although in his lifetime he achieved a rank above the minister level he was not committed to government service or political life. He was far more interested in academic pursuits especially the study of Confucian philosophy.

T'oegye worked in Seoul until 1569 with only a short three year break from 1549-52. In 1569 he retired and returned to his hometown to set up a private academy there for the study of Confucianism. He reportedly helped establish many other such schools in Korea. His first school, Tosan Sowon, was enlarged sometime after his death and still exists there. It has been designated as a historical site by the Korean government.

During his life, T'oegye used a number of pennames such as T'oedo, To-ong and Ch'ongnyang Sanin. After the death of his second wife, he took the name of T'oegye which happened to be the name of a pleasant stream meandering through his hometown.

T'oegye died on 8 December, 1570 (lunar calendar). His life spanned the reign of four kings and he held seven government positions. He also turned down many other offers of important positions in order to continue his studies. T'oegye had often retreated to his hometown to study in a quiet atmosphere. His motto was "Sincerity and Reverence" and he was known for living his life accordingly. He was canonized in the Temple of Confucius along with three other Korean sages during the reign of King Kwanghaegun in 1610.

Some of T'oegye's best known writings include; *Essays on Introspection (Chasongnok)*, *A Selective Collection of Chu Hsi's Letters (Chujaso Cholyo)* and *Neo-Confucianism (Songhak Sipto)*.

Many of his writings were later published in Japan and some noted Japanese scholars became disciples of T'oegye. In this sense he has had a significant impact on the Japanese development of Neo-Confucianism.

T'oegye is well respected in contemporary Korea. One of the major east-west running avenues in Seoul, T'oegye-ro, is named for him. Even more conspicuous is his picture which appears on the Korean 1,000 won note, Korea's most common note in circulation. On the reverse of it is a view of Tosan Sowon, his academy. The facility was remodeled in 1970 by President Park Chung-hee and is beautifully landscaped in the picturesque mountains northeast of Andong. The school consists of many buildings such as dormitories, other living quarters, and lecture halls where T'oegye once taught. His library is also preserved there containing 4,917 copies of 1,271 titles of his works. A small museum is attached which contains many of T'oegye's personal relics such as his walking stick, stool, mats, inkstone, etc., and a few of his works such as a collection of his poems, a record of his life, the register of the academy, some calligraphy and other collected works. In the center of Seoul, on the south side of Namsan Mountain stands a large statue of him. Through his many memorials, he is quietly present in the lives of many Koreans as they go about their daily routines.

23
Celebrated Sage and Confucian Philosopher
Yi Yi
(Yulgok, 1536-1584)

Yi Yi is a noted Korean sage. He is more commonly known by his penname Yulgok which means Chestnut Valley. He is most noted as a Confucian philosopher. Yulgok and T'oegye (see chapter 22) are the two most famous Korean Confucian Scholars. In addition to interpreting the works of previous Confucian scholars, Yulgok made famous his own views on Confucianism through his many writings.

Yulgok's early life was fortunate. He was born into an educated family. His father, Yi Won-su, was a scholar and a high government official. His mother, Shin Saimdang (see chapter 40), was well respected for her art works and her knowledge of the Chinese classics as well as poetry. Born on 26 December (lunar calendar) in Kangnung, Kangwon Province on the east coast of Korea, Yulgok started his education early. Most certainly owing to the help of his mother, he had completed his basic studies of the Confucian classics by the age of seven. He began writing poetry at the age of eight. By age thirteen he passed the literary civil service exams and became a *chinsa*, a kind of titled scholar. He continued his education by studying Buddhist scriptures and

Portrait of Yi Yi, celebrated sage and Confucian philosopher BOTTOM Ojuk'on, the birthplace of Yi Yi, and his famous mother Shin Saimdang

the Taoist classics. His brilliant mother died when he was only sixteen. Yulgok mourned for the traditional three years after which he spent a year in retreat in the Kumgang Mountains studying Zen Buddhism. Yulgok returned from the retreat to continue his Confucian studies. He also continued in the civil service examination process taking his last one at age twenty-nine. Along the way, in 1558, he met and married a governor's daughter. In the following year he went to visit the famous and respected sage, T'oegye. T'oegye was 35 years older than Yulgok and was a well established scholar and government official. T'oegye was impressed with young Yulgok's depth and intellect. Both men are believed to have come away from that meeting with a respect for each other that would last a lifetime. Yulgok deeply respected master T'oegye, even though in later years he would disagree with him on some fundamental philosophical points. In effect, they would become rivals even though they respected each other's work.

After he passed his final civil service exam he became eligible for government positions. Yulgok ascended through the ranks of government positions rising to the highest levels. In 1572, he decided to move to Haeju near the home of his wife's family. He was soon appointed governor there. The next year he became ill and resigned his position to retire to the little town of Yulgok from which he derived his penname. Over the next few years he completed a number of famous writings until, in 1576, he was appointed vice director of the Royal Academy. But again his government service did not last long before, a year later, he moved on to pursue more private academic matters. In 1582, just two years before his death he completed one of his most famous and important works, *A Key to Annihilating Ignorance (Kyongmong Yogyol)*. The next year he was appointed as the Minister of Justice and later Minister of Defense. He continued his writings throughout this period and died while serving as Defense Minister at the early age of forty-eight.

Yulgok lived during difficult times in Korean history. During his lifetime Korea had constant problems with marauding Japanese pirates and incursions across Korea's northern border by hostile invaders. He lived at least part of his life along with other giants of Korean history such as T'oegye and Admiral Yi Sun-shin. Much is written analyzing Yulgok's thought and comparing it to the thinking of other great philosophers. Far less is written about the man himself. This disciplined and dedicated scholar, statesman, philosopher, and family man has left a deep impression on Korea and on Confucian thought wherever in the world it is studied.

V

RELIGIOUS FIGURES

Han Yong-un

Kim Tae-gon

Samyongdang

24
Accomplished Poet, Monk and Independence Fighter

Han Yong-un
(Manhae, 1879–1944)

The life of this man of many faces is as interesting as it is varied. He was a farmer turned revolutionary turned monk turned independence fighter turned poet. Han was a man who followed his convictions and his convictions led him to great things. He is distinguished as one of the original signatories of the Korean Declaration of Independence from Japan on 1 March, 1919. He fought hard for the modernization and independence of Korea from Japan; unfortunately he never lived to see it. His father, Han Ung-jun, was a farmer in Ch'ungch'ong Province. Han was born there on 29 August in the village of Sobu-myon, Hongsong-gun. He was a second son and grew up in the small town rural atmosphere of the late nineteenth century Korea. As was the custom of that period, Han was initially schooled in the Chinese classics right in his own village. He grew up in the turmoil that was rapidly changing a country with a long history of traditional isolationism.

Government corruption and poverty of the peasants, during Han's childhood, had already caused several uprisings in Korea. It seemed conditions were worst in Cholla and

Han Yong-un, relentlessly struggled to provide the Korean people courage through his classic poetry

Ch'ungch'ong Provinces. Hoodlums and thieves were increasing in the countryside. Many peasants became followers of a new religion that began in the 1860's called Tonghak (Eastern Learning). In addition to religious views, Tonghak was a movement against government corruption, poor social and economic conditions, and unfair practices which caused suffering to the poor. Tonghak was also anti-Western, anti-Catholic and against the further domination of Korea by China. By 1892, the sect was strong and influential. A local persecution of the Tonghak in Han's province caused an uprising in 1892. Han became a follower himself and was deeply involved when a full rebellion erupted in 1894. The rebels captured the capital of Cholla Province, Chonju, and forced the government to offer a truce. However, the government, ultimately did not honor the truce and enlisted the aid of Chinese troops to quell the rebellion. This subsequently resulted in Japanese intervention and the Sino-Japanese War 1894-95. When Japan showed their military superiority over China the Korean government began to succumb to the domination of the Japanese. This changed the Tonghak focus to a struggle against Japan. Although they had some initial success, capturing Kongju, then the capital of Ch'ungch'ong Province, they were later badly beaten by Korean government and Japanese forces. Many followers were captured or went into hiding and the movement disintegrated by 1895. Han's father and brother were executed and Han, at the age of sixteen, went into hiding at a Buddhist temple.

Taking refuge in the Paektam temple near Sorak Mountain on the east coast, he studied Buddhism and other subjects. He became a priest in 1905 and adopted the pen name and Buddhist name Manhae, which means Ten Thousand Seas. He was a kind of reform Buddhist preaching a more socially involved Buddhism. Han encouraged monks to leave their temple enclaves and live among the poor helping to improve their conditions. He also advocated monks earning their own living and renouncing the vow of celibacy.

To increase his knowledge of Buddhism he traveled to Japan and met with counterpart scholars in 1909. For a time he studied at the Zen College of Komazawa near Tokyo. The following year when Japan annexed Korea, Han moved to Vladivostok and established an academy for the independence army.

Han returned to Korea and became a key figure in the independence movement. By 1919, he represented the Buddhist society when he signed the Declaration of Independence from Japan, on 1 March, along with thirty-two other patriots. In addition, Han supplemented the declaration with three principles, or pledges, that emphasized the non-violence of the movement. Shortly after its proclamation, many of the contributors, including Han, were arrested. The next three years (1920-23) Han spent in prison. In spite of the beatings and tortures, he spent spare moments writing letters and poems. His poems were inspiring and his works continued throughout his life. One poem, *Silence of My Sweetheart (Nimui Ch'immuk)*, is said to be not only one of his best compositions but a masterpiece of Korean poetry. Because of this and other important selections he is recognized as possibly, Korea's greatest modern poet.

This talented man, who contributed much to uplift the spirit of Koreans during a dark period of their history, died on 9 May, 1944. He had lived a full life leaving behind a wife and daughter in addition to the many political, religious and literary contributions he made in his sixty-five year life span.

25
First Christian Martyr

Kim Tae-gon
(1821–1846)

The first Christian martyr of Korea, Kim Tae-gon, sometimes called Father Kim or Andrew Kim, is remembered for his persistent efforts to spread Christianity on the peninsula. As is common with many martyrs, Kim led a short but eventful life which brought him the respect and admiration of his countrymen regardless of religious affiliation. Ch'ungch'ong Province was the birthplace of this future religious figure on 21 August (lunar calendar). He was a son in a family of martyrs. His father, Kim Che-jun, suffered as a martyr and died in 1839. His great grandfather, even though at one time a nobleman and government official, was persecuted and died in 1814 after many years in prison. In fact, the Kim family had to move to Kyonggi Province, sometime during Kim's youth, to avoid persecution.

The nineteenth century was riddled with Christian persecutions beginning as early as 1801. The early oppressions grew out of some basic conflicts between Christianity and Confucianism. One of the fundamental differences that precipitated the most emotion was the Christian disapproval of the Confucian ancestor worship. The obligation of offering

ABOVE Portrait of Kim Taegon (St. Andrew Kim)
RIGHT Statue of Father Kim located at the Choltusan Shrine in Seoul

sacrifices to deceased ancestors is deeply ingrained as a part of Korean society. Discouraging this practice and other basic Confucian rituals was perceived by many as disruptive to society and induced eventual persecutions of the Christians.

By the time Kim was eighteen years old another larger persecution occurred, which severely stalled the Korean Christian movement. His father was killed during this particular persecution. Kim was not in Korea at the time. Three years earlier he had entered the seminary, and in 1837, he left Korea to study in Macao at the Paris Foreign Mission Society. He tackled various subjects such as Latin, history, French and geography in addition to the traditional theology courses. Kim was forced to flee to the Philippines twice during his studies because of the Opium War in China (1840-42). Somehow he became an interpreter for French Admiral Cecile and was present at the Treaty of Nanking in 1842. As a result of the treaty, the city of Shanghai was opened to foreigners which in turn, allowed better access to missionaries there. Kim returned to China and for the next two years tried unsuccessfully to enter Korea through the northern border between the two countries. While in China, he was ordained a deacon, in 1844, and decided to enter Korea alone via a different route arriving in Seoul the following year.

Korea was in definite need of missionaries so Kim decided to return to China and escort some back to Seoul. When Kim reached Shanghai with his plan he was ordained the first Korean Catholic priest in August of 1845. He attempted to secretly return to Korea by boat, stopping first at Cheju Island, off the south coast, and then proceeding to Yonp'yong Island where Kim tried to arrange further transportation to the mainland. Unfortunately, he was arrested there in June 1846, and taken to prison in Seoul. He was beheaded some three months later, in September, at a military camp at Saenamt'o, near the Han River.

Christianity continued to spread, despite the attacks, and Christian persecutions continued throughout that century. During the rule of the Taewongun (see chapter 8), the year of 1866 witnessed a terrible rise in Catholic persecutions which lasted almost six years. In March of 1866, a decree to kill all Roman Catholics was announced. In great numbers, Catholics lost their property and either fled or lost their lives. Thousands were killed (many beheaded) at Choltusan overlooking the Han River in Seoul.

Today, some of Kim's writings and relics are displayed at the Catholic shrine and museum now at Choltusan, in Map'o-gu, on the west side of Seoul, along the Han River. A large bronze statue of Kim is also located there. The Catholic church has also constructed various memorials at Kim's birthplace in Naep'o about 100 kms south of Seoul near the city of Ch'onan. Many more relics and writings pertaining to him are displayed there.

26
Warrior Monk of the Yi Dynasty
Samyongdang
(Yujong, 1544-1610)

Remembered as a warrior monk, in the mid Yi Dynasty (1392-1910), Samyongdang developed into an important religious figure, politician and even diplomat. He recruited his own forces to battle Korea's foreign enemies and both fought against and was an envoy to the Japanese. Like many famous characters, his career went through a tragic period when he fell from favor and later returned to prominence. More than four hundred years after his birth he is still remembered as a distinguished character of Korean history.

The little town of Miryang in South Kyongsang Province was Samyongdang's birthplace. Miryang is just south of the border with North Kyongsang Province and near the major city of Taegu. He grew up there and spent a large portion of his life in the area within a one hundred kilometer circle of Taegu.

At the early age of thirteen, Samyongdang moved to the now famous Chikchisa Buddhist Temple roughly sixty kilometers northeast of Taegu. There he studied Buddhism and became a monk, taking the name "Samyongdang." Some four years later, in 1561, he passed the national Buddhist

TOP **Portrait of Samyongdang** ABOVE **Haeinsa Temple southwest of Taegu, where Samyongdang stayed until his death**

monk examination and continued to progress as a Buddhist scholar. By 1575, at the age of thirty-one, Samyongdang had developed much respect within the Son sect (sometimes known by the Japanese name of Zen sect) of Buddhism. That year he was offered a position as the head of the Son sect but humbly refused preferring instead to live a simple life as a common monk. He continued to live a respectable but ordinary life for some years until outside events introduced tragedy and disrupted his life.

The Yi Dynasty of the mid sixteenth century was showing many signs of decay. Factionalism had arisen between the orthodox and Neo-Confucian scholars in addition to distrust and disagreement which developed between the king and the government bureaucracy. In 1562, Yi Dynasty Korea witnessed its first peasant rebellion which occured in Hwanghae Province. The rebellion was suppressed at the cost of many lives and much property damage. In time a more serious rebellion was plotted by Chong Yo-rip, an educated government official who belonged to a faction of confucian scholars known as the Eastern Men. His plot was discovered in 1589, and many of his followers and conspirators were imprisoned or killed. The government was fearful of another rebellion and took great pains to arrest anyone who may have been involved. Samyongdang was associated with the conspiracy and was arrested even though he claimed innocence. The rebellion was mainly associated within the Cholla Province, which had little relation to Samyongdang. After some time in prison he was finally exonerated and released.

About this time Japan, under the leadership of Toyotomi Hideyoshi, was planning to attack Ming Dynasty China. Originally they desired to use Korea as a springboard but could not persuade Korea to help them or allow their troops passage. So in 1592, Hideyoshi invaded Korea with 160,000 troops. The invasion was initially a smashing success with the first troops landing at Pusan in April and marching north to Taegu and Ch'ongju that month and capturing Seoul in May and Pyongyang in June. Koreans fought back however, and the war lasted seven years and consisted of two such coordinated attacks from Japan. Samyongdang was quick to react and formed Buddhist forces to repel the invaders. Samyongdang became the deputy general of the forces and helped lead them into battle. In 1593, he became the commander of his forces and also received a high government position for his successful resistance against the Japanese. From 1594, he ordered three fortresses built in the vicinity of Taegu. The largest, P'algong Fortress was due north of Taegu, the second and somewhat smaller was Kumo Fortress, about 30 kilometers northwest of Taegu near Kumi City, and the last was Yonggi Fortress, about 40 kilometers west of Taegu in the Kaya Mountains.

Many heroes emerged during the war with Japan including one of Korea's most famous, Admiral Yi Sun-shin, (see chapter 20). With the efforts of many dedicated soldiers like Samyongdang coupled with the smashing naval victories of Admiral Yi, the Japanese were forced to end their advance and eventually withdraw in 1598.

The war was not completely over however, for either Korea or Samyongdang. The Japanese had taken many prisoners of war which had not as yet been released. In 1602, Samyongdang had received a government position as a District Governor, and in 1604, King Sonjo called upon him to act as special envoy to Japan to negotiate the release of prisoners. His efforts were again very successful and by the following year he had completed negotiations for the release of three thousand prisoners.

For the next few years he lived quietly until he became quite ill and could not recover well. He moved to Haeinsa Buddhist temple in 1610, in hope to aid his recuperation in the beautiful Kaya Mountains. Unfortunately he did not recover and died there that same year.

Today, the three fortresses he ordered built in Kyongsang Province are national parks. Chikchisa Temple, where he studied and became a Buddhist monk is still a thriving temple and somewhat of a tourist attraction. The temple boasts a famous portrait of Samyongdang and a hall commemorating him. Haeinsa Temple, where he died, is also a famous and thriving temple. This famous spot appropriately displays a monument in honor of this important and distinguished character.

VI

BUSINESSMEN

Chung Ju-yung

Kim Woo-choong

27
Tireless Business Tycoon

Chung Ju-yung
(1915-)

One of Korea's remarkable business success stories, this rags to riches business tycoon used his personal knack for opportunity, combined with boldness and hardwork, to build a business empire, the Hyundai Company. Chung rode the wave of Korea's economic success for the three decades beginning in the 1960's and expanded his company into a world class business giant. More recently, in his senior years, he became a formidable political candidate forming his own political party and preparing himself as a presidential candidate. He appears as a man that has done it all, or could do it all if he so desired, and his accomplishments have made him legendary, even if sometimes controversial, throughout Korea.

A small village in Asan, Kangwon Province was his birthplace on 15 November, 1915. His father was a simple farmer but was able to provide the basic education necessary to all young children of that period. Chung studied the basic Chinese characters until he was ten years old, then entered a local primary school and completed it some five years later. This was all the formal education this future billionaire

Chung Ju-yung, founder of Hyundai Group, one of the largest conglomerates in Korea

would receive. As the oldest son of eight children, his father expected him to take over the family farm that had been the family trade for some generations. Chung had other ideas however, and at a very young age, ran away to Wonsan, in present day North Korea, to find his own way. He took various odd jobs there requiring heavy labor on construction sites building roads and railways. Even though the work was hard and the days long Chung continued his education at a local school. This soon ended when his father found him and brought him back home to help on the farm. By the time he was nineteen he was itching to be on his own again and this time slipped away to Seoul, by train, with the little money he had saved. He languished a short time, unable to find work there, and traveled to Inch'on, Korea's second largest port city, where he found work on the docks. After a while, he returned to Seoul and obtained a job, as a delivery boy, at a rice mill in Insa-dong. Chung advanced in the company, eventually working there as a bookkeeper where he gained valuable basic business knowledge. Armed with his newfound knowledge and a lot of ambition, he opened his own rice store in Seoul which was small but successful. He was forced to return home, however, when the Japanese colonial government's rice rationing system forced him out of business.

At age twenty-five, he returned to Seoul and began an auto repair business in Puk-ahyon-dong. Initial success turned to tragedy when a fire burned down his business and left him again in debt. With indefatigable determination he later opened another garage on the east side of Seoul in Shinsol-dong. Again his business was successful and, by Korean liberation in 1945, he had made enough money to move his family to Seoul with him. This time his fortune was more permanent and Chung opened a bigger shop in Wonhyo-ro, called Hyundai Auto Repair Company, coining the company name he would retain throughout his business life.

Although his auto business was good, he remembered, from his days as a laborer, that the construction business was the most profitable. In 1950, Chung established the Hyundai Construction Company, which over the years has grown into a world class business. Hyundai landed some large construction projects which earned him the trust of, then president, Rhee Syng-man. Under the Rhee administration, Hyundai was rewarded with large construction projects such as the rebuilding of the Han River Bridge, destroyed during the Korean War. During the subsequent Park administration beginning in 1961, Chung impressed the president and received many important contracts to rebuild Korea with needed facilities such as dams, power stations and major highways. Hyundai Construction was chosen to build the Seoul-Pusan Expressway, the main road linking the capital with the country's largest port. In the late 60's and early 70's, with great foresight, Chung expanded his projects to the Middle East, boldly succeeding against the predictions of many "experts." About the same time, Chung steered Hyundai into the shipbuilding industry. Again, without much experience, he was able to turn this venture into an impressive success. Later, he expanded into the automotive and electronics industries where he continued to achieve impressive results.

Long recognized as a successful businessman Chung was elected Chairman of the Federation of Korean Industries, in 1977, and was subsequently elected to four more two-year terms. In order to repay his country for his good fortune he established the Asan Foundation, in 1977, by transferring a large portion of Hyundai stocks to help fund it. The foundation sponsors scholarships for research and concentrates on improving health care for the underprivileged, especially in remote country areas.

With an envious business success record Chung decided to enter politics in the 1992 National Assembly elections. The Unification National Party, which he helped form, did surprisingly well in the elections and had its sights set on the Presidency in 1992 with the aggressive senior citizen at its helm. Chung was defeated in the election, however, he is still forceful and energetic even at seventy-eight.

Married to Byun Joong-suk, in 1938, when she was only sixteen, Chung has fathered eight children. Tremendous success has not spoiled Chung and his wife however, as they still live in a rather ordinary home in downtown Seoul near Kyongbok Palace. The title of his autobiography, *Many Trials But No Failures*, provides insight into the philosophy of this character which is at once complex and ordinary. Unyielding determination and hard work have served him well and earned him a place as one of the most successful businessmen in Korea's history.

28
The Living Legend of Business
Kim Woo-choong
(1936 -)

One of Korea's most successful and hardest charging businessmen, Kim is well-known and respected in Korea and the world business community. The founding and development of Daewoo Corporation is one of his most noted achievements. From almost nothing he built one of the largest and most successful companies in the history of Korea. His story can be, in many ways, inspiring to aspiring entrepreneurs.

Early life for Kim was somewhat difficult. Although born to an educated family as the third son on 19 December, 1936, by the time he reached his teens the Korean War had devastated his family. Kim's father had been kidnapped and his mother and older brother went into hiding while his oldest brother was attending the Korean military academy. Kim, at the age of 14, was forced to try and provide for the family. He did so by taking odd jobs such as selling vegetables or peddling newspapers. Moving around as dictated by the dynamics of the war, Kim spent most of his time in Taegu living on the edge of poverty with part of his family. After the war, Kim moved back to Seoul ahead of his family and continued studying. He graduated from Kyonggi High

Kim Woo-jung, Daewoo Group's founder and one of the most successful businessmen in Korea

School and entered Yonsei University, on a scholarship, to study economics in 1956. He used this time not only to develop his education but to cement personal relationships with classmates who would later rise with him in the business world.

Kim's first real introduction to business came after college when he took a temporary management position at Hansong Industrial Company. He did well and was given a permanent position there in 1961. Kim executed some daring business deals which helped propel the company to financial success. Kim was promoted and it was during this period, in 1964, that he married Chung Hee-ja. Eager for continued advancement and willing to take risks, Kim accepted an offer from a friend at Daetoe Textile Company to start a joint venture. Kim borrowed about $18,000 to start the company. They decided to call their new company Daewoo. They took the Dae from Daetoe Textile and the Woo from Kim's name, the combination, Daewoo, taking on the entirely new meaning of "Grand Universe." The company was created on 22 March, 1967 when Kim was only 30 years old.

The formation of Daewoo was fortuitously timed with Korea's drive to become an export economy. Daewoo quickly collected orders for textile exports of $580,000 in its first year. The next year Daewoo built its own factory and increased export sales to $2.9 million. Daewoo diversified and expanded and by 1971 had raised its exports to over $24 million. The company soon won major contracts with some giant U.S. retailers like Sears, J. C. Penney, and K-Mart. By 1972, Daewoo became Korea's second largest exporter with almost $53 million in exports. Over the next few years, Daewoo continued to expand and started acquiring other companies which had not been as successful. In 1977, Kim completed the Daewoo center building in downtown Seoul across from the Seoul train station, which was the largest office building in Korea at that time. By 1978 he finally reached his goal of becoming Korea's number one exporter beating out Samsung Company by exporting over $705 million. His company held this title for four straight years by eventually breaking through the $1 billion export mark. In a mere eleven years Kim had brought his company to the top of the business world. From textiles and wigs to autos, electronics and shipbuilding the growth of Daewoo was truly an extraordinary accomplishment.

Kim's personal work habits are legendary. He rarely takes a day off or a vacation and he only took three days off for his honeymoon. He reportedly sleeps and average of four–five hours a night, catching naps on airplanes or in cars on the way to appointments. In 1984, *Fortune* magazine wrote an article labeling him the hardest worker in South Korea. The article highlighted Kim's incredible seven days a week 15 hours a day schedule. Much of Kim's assets have been donated to charity. He has sponsored various foundations and scholarship funds over which he maintains no financial control. Kim reportedly lives modestly in Seoul with his family. His wife studied at Harvard and is the chairwoman of a Daewoo subsidiary which owns the Seoul Hilton Hotel. He has three children.

The book he wrote in 1989 titled *It's a Big World and There's a Lot to Do*, became an almost immediate best seller with over a million copies sold in the first few months. Kim has turned almost every project into success. He is respected in Korea and internationally as a hardworking businessman and a generous and compassionate man.

VII

SCHOLARS

Chi Sok-yong

Ch'oe Che-u

Ch'oe Ch'i-won

Chong In-bo

Chong Mong-ju

Chong Yak-yong

Kim Chong-hui

Pang Chong-hwan

29
Medical Missionary

Chi Sok-yong
(1855 –1935)

Scholar, medical doctor, and philanthropist, Chi was a man dedicated to improving the health and welfare of Korean people through his knowledge of medicine and his belief in the value of education. He was most famous for his efforts to eradicate smallpox in Korea.

Born in Nagwon-dong, in central Seoul, little is written about his youth growing up in the capital. He was influenced by an educated man, Pak Yong-son, who became Chi's teacher and mentor. Pak was the translator to Kim Ki-su, who led an official Korean mission to Japan in 1876 to learn as much as possible about Japan's modernization. Pak's stories of Japan, especially their advances in Western medicine, must have interested young Chi as he decided to travel to Pusan and study medicine at the Japanese Naval Hospital in 1879. There he learned the benefits of vaccination to the overall health of people and prevention of diseases.

In December of the same year, Chi returned to his wife's hometown of Doksan-myon, Ch'ungju, North Ch'ungch'ong Province, to provide vaccinations and medical treatment to local villagers. In 1880, he expanded his services to include

Chi Sok-yong, completely dedicated to the health and welfare of the Korean people

Seoul and continued to apply Japanese knowledge, of how to manufacture and administer vaccinations, to the medical problems in Korea.

The spread of Japanese influence in Korea, in the late 1800's, was troubling for many citizens and by 1882, a military revolt erupted, known as Imo Kullan, which ultimately resulted in the Taewongun (see chapter 8) taking power. The Taewongun took advantage of the revolt to encourage a wave of anti-Japanese agitation which resulted in the persecution of many pro-Japanese thinkers including Chi. Because of this environment, and the threat of arrest, Chi fled south to the countryside. By September of 1882, the governor of Cholla Province requested Chi help initiate vaccination programs in Chonju and other cities. Chi set up a vaccination bureau in Cholla Province and was active in teaching vaccination theory and instructing methods of administering vaccinations to the needy. The following year he set up a similar program in Kongju.

In 1883, he passed the government civil service examinations and continued his work and research in medicine. Two years later, he finished his book, *New Theories About Vaccination*, and was well on his way to becoming well-known for his extensive work in this field. As with many famous people, tragedy struck his career when in 1887, he was identified as part of a pro-Japanese, anti-government political party and exiled to Shinjido, an island in Cholla Province. He stayed there for four years until his release in 1891. In that same year, he returned to Seoul and established a small school teaching about vaccinations. Because of his talent and reputation, and the fact that he had previously passed the civil service examinations, he was eligible for government service. He received an appointment as a district chief near the port city of Pusan on the southeast coast of Korea.

In 1899, Chi returned to Seoul and became the Dean of Kyongsong Medical School for some ten years. From this post he became interested in the spread of literacy and was a proponent of using the Korean alphabet *(han-gul)* over

Chinese characters. Chi believed in a wider use of *han-gul* in official documents that had traditionally been prepared in Chinese characters. He went on to establish a *han-gul* institute, Kuk-mun Institute, in Seoul in 1908, to study the Korean language. Within a year, he wrote the *Chajon Sokyo*, which is a kind of dictionary of the Korean language, which was much needed at that time. Chi continued his work until his death.

He is remembered as a man who gave much of himself in devotion to others. His tireless dedication to the health and education of needy Koreans improved the lives of many fortunate individuals and made him one of the most well-known figures in modern Korean history.

30
Founder of the Tonghak Movement

Ch'oe Che-u
(Suun, 1824-1864)

Great opportunity comes to few men and even fewer are prepared to take advantage at the proper moment. Ch'oe was a man with ambition and was wise enough to recognize the chance to achieve his goals. Prepared to seize the opportunity at the right moment, he was able, for a brief period of history, to rise from a lowly existence to a leader of a major nationalist religious movement in Korea. Tonghak, the movement he founded, swept through much of southern Korea in the mid nineteenth century. It grew strong enough to outlive its founder and influence the history of Korea.

Ironically, the man who would become famous in the southwestern province of Cholla, and whose religion would later spark serious rebellions there, was born in the southeastern province of Kyongsang, a traditional rival. The little town of Kajong-ri, near Kyongju was his birthplace on 18 October, 1824. Although his family was not well-off at the time they were very proud of their ancestry. His noble lineage could be traced back twenty-eight generations to the famous Shilla Dynasty scholar, Ch'oe Ch'i-won (see chapter 31). Unfortunately for Ch'oe, his early life was somewhat

Ch'oe Che-u, founder of Tonghak, the largest indigenous religion of Korea. Ch'oe amalgamated the main precepts of various traditional philosophies to form the foundation of his religion

unlucky. His father, Ch'oe Ok, was a poor man of the educated class who was a local teacher. When Ch'oe was only six years old his mother died. Since his mother had been a concubine his birth carried somewhat of a stigma in Yi Dynasty Korea. This social blemish brought constant disappointment to his aspirations. By the time he was thirteen, his marriage had been arranged and only three years later his father died. Life for the young man did not seem to offer much promise. Young Ch'oe had a strong desire to achieve fame similar to his great ancestors. Sometime after a final bout with misfortune in 1844, when fire destroyed much of his home and most of the family library, he left his hometown and traveled to his wife's native village of Ulsan, arriving the following year. There he studied Chinese and Korean classics for about ten years. At the age of thirty-one, and still with not much to show for his life, he met a Buddhist monk who helped him find his spiritual self. For the next four years he studied, prayed and meditated near Yangsan, on Ch'onsong mountain in Kyongsang Province. He finally returned to his hometown in 1859.

Although there were only five years left in his life he still had not achieved any great fame. Matters would change quickly, however, as Korea would become indignant by the spread of Western religions and Western influence in Korea and the desire of many people to counterbalance that growth. Sometime in 1860, Ch'oe had a vision that convinced him he was divinely chosen to lead the people out of the old Confucian stagnation and corruption and away from the appeal of the Western religions. He founded Tonghak (Eastern Learning) as a synthesis of some parts of Confucianism, Taoism, and Buddhism.

At first, Tonghak was not accepted well in his own village so Ch'oe went on a mission to Cholla Province where his teachings started to take root. The farmers and peasants of Korea were attracted to Tonghak's egalitarianism which was in sharp contrast to the social pressures and inequality they experienced under the strictly vertical Confucian society. Within a few years he could boast of chapters in virtually all parts of Cholla Province and throughout southern Korea. This religious movement was as much anti-government as it was anti-foreign and as a result quickly became a social problem for the government. Members of the Tonghak were plentiful and their tolerance for the corruption and abuse of the local government officials had worn thin. Uprisings began in Chinju in 1862, which forced the king to order reform measures aimed at curbing government corruption, but the reform measures were mostly ineffective and the unrest continued to spread. The government was forced to arrest Ch'oe and many of his followers in 1863. Choe was sent to Taegu and executed there the following year.

The death of Ch'oe could not completely stop the spread of Tonghak. A new leader, Ch'oe Shi-hyong, quickly took his place, but that same year other political events caused the movement to become temporarily dormant. King Ch'olchong died and the new king, Kojong, was too young to rule so his father, the Taewongun, ruled as his regent. Taewongun was very strict and oppression flourished throughout his reign. However, the Tonghak would appear again in the 1890's even stronger than before. They would become a military force with grass-roots support, initially capturing various cities before being "reckoned with" by Chinese troops which were called in to help suppress the Tonghak Rebellion of 1894.

In the end, the Tonghak hastened the conflict between Japan and China for suzerainty over Korea. Ironically, the movement Ch'oe founded to rid Korea of foreign influence and control actually precipitated both. The Korea he sought to change would, in fact, never be the same, but in a much different way than he had intended.

31
Great Sage of the Shilla Dynasty

Ch'oe Ch'i-won
(857–?)

One of the most famous scholars of the Shilla period, Ch'oe, as was many scholars of that time, was also highly regarded as a calligrapher, poet, writer and philosopher. He has the peculiar distinction of being the founder of his clan and was the first Korean to be honored by acceptance, as a sage, into the Sunggyungwan Academy. He was a prolific writer and many of his works are still available.

Ch'oe was born late in the Shilla Dynasty and was alive during the decline of that dynasty and probably lived to see the rise of the succeeding Koryo Dynasty. He was fortunate enough to travel to China to study at the age of twelve and he reportedly became a master of Chinese learning in a very short time. His work in composing Chinese letters was lauded and he was able to pass the Chinese Tang Dynasty civil service examinations at the early age of seventeen. Ch'oe stayed in China for another eleven years working as an official in various government positions. In 874, the same year he passed his government exams, he became a sheriff in a local community. Five years later, he received a position as a kind of inspector of government officials, ensuring they con-

Portrait of Ch'oe Ch'i-won, who was respected as a scholar in China as well as in Korea

ducted themselves properly, consistent with good manners and official customs. In that same year, he was appointed as an aid to the commander of military forces dispatched to quell a local rebellion. He eventually did well enough to receive the title of ambassador. Finally, in 885, he returned home to Shilla Dynasty Korea, young but learned and with much experience from China that afforded him respect at home.

The Shilla Dynasty of the late ninth century experienced much turmoil and decline. The peasants had, for years, been overworked and heavily taxed to pay for the extravagances of the aristocracy. Thieves and robbers were rampant in the countryside and the government was ineffective in dealing with them. By 887, during the reign of Queen Chinsong, rebellion broke out in several areas. This led to the formation of the Later Paekche Kingdom in the southwest and the Later Koguryo Kingdom in the north central region of the peninsula. This brief period was known as the Later Three Kingdoms period and persisted until Wang Kon (see chapter 13), again unified the country in 936, and formed the new Koryo Dynasty. Ironically, many of these later uprisings were either started or supported by prominent men who had received their training in China and, in a sense, Ch'oe was in this group.

After receiving his training in China, Ch'oe returned to a high position in the Shilla government as a *hallim haksa* or a preparer of royal decrees. He had a firm grasp of the problems plaguing the government bureaucracy and had some definite notions on how to correct them. Ch'oe and two other influential scholars; Ch'oe Sung-u and Ch'oe Shin-ji, were active in the reform movement during this period. Ch'oe was disappointed with the old Bone Rank System which rewarded bloodline over merit. He wanted to effect changes in the government that would enable men of ability to prosper along with men of nobility. Ch'oe carefully prepared a letter (Ten Issues of the Day) to Queen Chinsong describing what he felt were the most consequential topics for the government to address. When his suggestions were not taken seriously he became disillusioned with the system, but unlike many of his comrades who turned to violent revolution, he retreated to his studies in the quiet serenity of Mount Kaya, in the southern part of Korea, after a period of visiting various temples. There he more earnestly began a level of writing that earned him the often heard name of "Father of Korean Literature." Unfortunately, relatively few of his works still exist in comparison to the incredible number of works he completed. His most famous extant works include *Kyewon P'ilgyong* and *Chungsan Pokkwejip*.

The last part of Choe's life is still a mystery that includes many legends and unanswered questions. He disappeared quite strangely and no one knows for sure how, when or where he died.

It is written that Ch'oe was the founder of his clan. The family name of Ch'oe was awarded to the chief of one of the six tribes that originally joined to form the Shilla kingdom approximately 37 B.C. From that family of Ch'oe's, many clans were formed based on geographical location. Ch'oe Ch'i-won was the founder of the Kyongju Ch'oe clan.

He is remembered for his calligraphy and scholarly pursuits. He was an accomplished writer and poet with the highest academic credentials. As a reformer, he was not as successful, but he did not appear to persist where he could not prevail. He lived his own way ignoring the violent changes that were developing around him. In the end, the memory of his accomplishments outlived the events that transpired and his fame has transcended the petty rivalries and squabbles of his era.

32
Dedicated Historian

Chong In-bo
(1892 – ?)

Scholar, patriot and dedicated government official, Chong is most remembered as an accomplished Korean historian. His efforts to keep Korean history alive during the Japanese colonial period caused him much difficulty. However, his persistence, and solid reputation for honesty and integrity landed him an important government position after the liberation of Korea, and an honored place in Korean history. He was reportedly kidnapped to North Korea during the Korean War and was never heard from again.

Born in Seoul, Chong came from a proud ancestral heritage. His most famous ancestor was probably his great grandfather, Chong Won-yong, who was a prime minister during the reign of Yi Dynasty, King Ch'olchong (1849-1863). From an early age, Chong reportedly had a love for reading and writing, and by thirteen years old he was surprising local residents with his *shijo*, Korean poetry. When Japan annexed Korea in 1910, Chong left Korea to study in China. While there, he helped establish a group in Shanghai called the Mutual Assistance Society (Tongjesa), for the purpose of educating Koreans and inspiring nationalism with the hope

Chong In-bo, man of many talents including scholar, patriot, journalist and historian. He struggled for Korean independence

of liberating his country. He worked closely with other famous Koreans such as Shin Ch'ae-ho (see chapter 46), and Shin Kyu-shik. The Tongjesa, later joined with the Chinese Guomindang to form a Korean-Chinese partnership known as the New Mutual Assistance Society (Shin Tongjesa). About the same time, Chong, in cooperation with Shin Ch'ae-ho and others, established the Paktal Academy which educated Korean youth living in China.

In 1918, just before the Korean independence movement, he returned to Korea. He continued his nationalist efforts and, within a few years, became a professor of Korean and Oriental history at Yonhui University, the predecessor of today's Yonsei University. He also held a position as professor at what has become Ewha Womans University. Through the rest of the Japanese occupation he continued to record and publish articles and books on Korean history. At one point he obtained a position on the *Dong-A Ilbo* newspaper editorial committee. In 1931, he published a series of articles in the *Dong-A Ilbo* titled "The Korean Spirit for Five Thousand Years." These articles were later published as a book titled, *A Study on Korean History*. His version of Korean history conflicted with that of the Japanese and caused much difficulty for Chong with the Japanese colonial government.

Threatened by possible arrest for his anti-Japanese writings and activities, Chong moved to Iksan, North Cholla Province until Korea was finally liberated at the end of World War II. He returned to Seoul in 1946, and, within two years, was given a post similar to an Attorney General, as the director of a special inspection committee in the new South Korean Government. He later founded and became dean of a national history college, continuing the tradition of researching and publishing works on Korean history.

Sometime after the outbreak of the Korean War, Chong was kidnapped to North Korea and was never heard from again. However his dedication to his country and his devotion to education of the Korean people continues to be remembered.

33
Loyal Koryo Statesman

Chong Mong-ju
(P'oun, 1337–1392)

Faithful statesman and Neo-Confucian scholar of the Koryo Dynasty, P'oun rose to high office in the late Koryo period. He became an envoy to Ming Dynasty China and Japan and favorably impressed officials there. He was a respected member of the faculty at the national academy, Songgyungwan University, and is often referred to as one of the fathers of Neo-Confucianism in Yi Dynasty Korea. He experienced problems however, when he would not swear complete loyalty to the founder of the Yi Dynasty which eventually cost him his life by way of a famous assassination.

P'oun passed the civil service examinations at age twenty-three and became an instructor in Neo-Confucianism at Songgyungwan University in 1367. At that time, the national university was located in the Koryo Dynasty capital of Kaesong. It had been there since 1308 and would remain there until the founder of the Yi Dynasty would move it to his new capital, Seoul, in 1398. Along with other famous scholars such as Yi Saek, P'oun taught at Songgyungwan while holding a government position. P'oun, and others,

RIGHT Portrait of Chong Mong-ju
BOTTOM RIGHT The historic bridge where he was tragically assassinated
BOTTOM LEFT A sample of his famous calligraphy

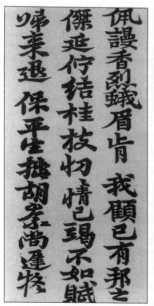

helped establish the Chinese classics as the core curriculum, and emphasized the interpretations of Chu Hsi. His writings and other scholarly efforts brought him great respect in the Koryo court. The Koryo Dynasty was experiencing severe turbulence in the late fourteenth century and would come to rely on P'oun who performed some brilliant diplomacy which temporarily helped the ailing dynasty. Unfortunately for P'oun, he had attached himself to a sinking ship that could not be saved by his efforts alone.

Problems plagued the Koryo Kingdom, during this period, from several different perspectives. Japanese pirates had been a persistent problem, appearing and disappearing at will, raiding and menacing the coastal areas for many years. Koryo had been ineffective in dealing with the pirates or their Japanese neighbors to the east. To the west, the Mongol Yüan Dynasty in China had been driven out by the new Ming Dynasty in 1368. While the Mongols had been displaced they were not powerless and still maintained some significant forces possibly large enough to attempt a comeback. This caused severe division in the Koryo court between pro-Mongol and pro-Ming factions. In 1374, Koryo King Kongmin died and was replaced by young King Shinu. Ming China did not immediately recognize the new king but the Mongols were quick to in hopes of gaining Koryo assistance against the Ming. Anti-Ming forces within the Koryo government quickly gained power and pro-Ming officials such as P'oun were removed. King Shinu himself was almost a pawn in the hardball politics that was unfolding in his court. He reportedly paid more attention to his own personal pleasures than to the affairs of state which had been taken over by one of his key officials, Yi In-im. The anti-Ming attitude of Koryo was already developing into serious problems, between the two countries, when one Ming emissary was killed on his way back to China. Koryo sent one delegation to try and smooth out this serious incident but the delegation was treated rudely and rebuked by the Ming court. Koryo ultimately called upon P'oun to travel to China to attempt reconciliation and he was very successful. Soon after, the Mongols began demanding Koryo assistance against the Ming and Mongol forces started posturing in the north. Koryo sent forces to counter them in 1376, but at the same time, was having extreme difficulties dealing with Japanese pirates who had become more bold and had even advanced inland to capture the city of Kongju. P'oun was again called on to approach the Japanese Shogun and ask for assistance in eliminating the pirates. Again P'oun succeeded where no one else could, traveling to Japan, making a favorable impression on the Japanese and receiving a promise of assistance. Unfortunately, the Japanese were not very effective either in dealing with the pirates and it took the efforts of two famous Koryo generals, Ch'oe Yong, and Yi Song-gye to turn back their advance and eventually defeat them.

The Ming emperor viewed the Koryo situation with much disfavor and began demanding tribute from Koryo which was more than Koryo could afford, and in 1385, P'oun again traveled to China with a peace offering and was able to win some favor with the emperor. Later, in 1386, the Ming emperor finally formally recognized the Koryo king. Koryo adopted Ming dress and customs and continued good relations until 1388 when the Ming moved to acquire some northern Koryo territories. The Koryo king ordered an expedition against the Ming but General Yi Song-gye, who had started out on the expedition, decided to turn his forces around and use them to take control of his own government.

Although Yi removed the old government he did not ascend the throne right away even though the common people were in favor of it. The leader of the opposition to Yi was P'oun himself, who was fiercely loyal to the displaced Koryo Dynasty. P'oun was revered by many in Korea, including Yi, but he had become an obstacle to progress and had to be removed for the Yi Dynasty to actually consolidate and prosper. Yi gave a party for P'oun and afterward, on his way home, P'oun was murdered by five men on the Sonjukkyo Bridge in Kaesong. This bridge has now become a monument and it is said that a stain of his blood is a brown spot on one of the stones which, to this day, reportedly turns red when it rains. Thus ended the life of one of the most loyal and respected Koryo officials of his era. He was the personification of Confucian loyalty even at the cost of his own life. He was honored in 1517, 125 years after his death, when he was canonized into the national academy with other Korean sages such as Ch'oe Ch'i-won, Yulgok and T'oegye, to name a few.

34
Practical Philosopher

Chong Yak-yong
(Tasan, 1762-1836)

One of the most eminent scholars in Korean History, Tasan, had a distinguished career which included accomplishments in history, poetry, political philosophy, science and engineering. Not just an intellectual, Tasan is known for his ability to apply his knowledge to help people. He is most well-known as the founder of *Shirhak* (Practical Learning).

He was born in the little village of Mahyon, north of the present boundaries of Seoul. His family was of the privileged class and his father, Chong Chae-won, was a local magistrate. Tasan's father was later appointed to a government position in Seoul and the family moved down to the city when Tasan was only fourteen, and he was married the same year. Tasan was schooled in the traditional Chinese and Korean classics but had an interest in Western teachings including Western religions.

Before he passed the civil service examinations in 1780 he was exposed to European studies, math, astronomy, Western customs, and Christian religions.

After passing his exams and entering government service, Tasan quickly made a name for himself by completing

Chong Yak-yong, this distinguished scholar used his knowledge to help others

some important public projects. When Tasan was merely thirty years old he designed and supervised the building of the high stone walls that fortified the city of Suwon. To do this cheaply and more effectively he utilized a windlass, which is a special kind of crane he invented, that was capable of lifting heavy stones easily. Much of those walls are still standing in Suwon today.

Tasan held many other positions such as royal reader to the king, secret inspector of Kyonggi Province, instructor at the famous Songgyungwan University in Seoul, magistrate, assistant minister of defense, and assistant minister of justice. Early in his career, when he was the reader for King Chongjo, he quickly became the favorite of the king and was known as the best reader in the palace. This relationship gave Tasan important access and he was frequently asked for advice from the monarch, who was considered one of the enlightened kings.

Trouble soon befell Tasan however, when King Chongjo died in 1801. Tasan had become a Catholic in 1784 and was caught in the Catholic persecutions of 1801. He was exiled first to Kyongsang Province then to Kangjin, in Cholla Province, for seventeen years, until 1818. In 1808, he moved to Kyol-dong, near a mountain known as Tasan, (hence his pen name) which means "tea mountain." It was during this exile that he penned some of his most famous works and arose as an ardent advocate of *Shirhak*.

This practical learning, *Shirhak*, was in clear contrast with the old Confucian ideals of the Yi Dynasty (1392-1910). *Shirhak* scholars, including Tasan, proposed new utilitarian ways to deal with national problems. Tasan also proposed new concepts for Korean government that demanded good government as an obligation of officials to the people and not a favor granted from the privileged class to the poor unfortunates. He wrote two important books on politics which addressed the systemic problems permeating the government and provided some possible solutions. He expanded his writings to other subjects including geography, economics, medicine, education and agriculture. As a poet,

Tasan was prolific. In fact, he is believed to have composed some 2,500 poems which is more than any other individual in Korea's history. He and the other *Shirhak* scholars were successful, in many respects, at inducing reform in the late Yi Dynasty.

After his exile, Tasan retired to his home in Yangju. He refused offers of government positions to continue his studies. Tasan died in 1836 and is buried in the country village of Majae, in Namyangju-gun, northeast of Seoul. There is a color portrait of Tasan and a landscape painting by Tasan located in the small museum at Choltusan. This shrine, in honor of Catholic martyrs who died in Seoul during persecutions in the nineteenth century, is located on the west side of Seoul facing the Han River. There is also a large bronze statue of Tasan on Namsan mountain in the center of Seoul. Most of the relics and writings pertaining to this great man are kept at a museum in Kangjin, on the southwestern coast of Korea. This prominent thinker, scholar and reformer made a permanent impression on his country. Even after his death, his concepts were thought to have influenced later reformers involved in other movements of the 1890's. He was clearly ahead of his time and will be remembered for his dedication to modernize and improve his country.

35
Master Calligrapher

Kim Chong-hui
(Ch'usa, 1786 –1856)

One of the most famous calligraphers of Korea, Ch'usa developed and made famous his own style of calligraphy. His talent extended far beyond this however, into painting, poetry and philosophy. His travels brought him in contact with great scholars from China, at an early age, which helped accelerate his own development. Many of his works are still extant and he is remembered as a complete scholar known for his depth and originality.

As a descendant of a high ranking Koryo Dynasty family, Ch'usa benefited from additional privileges that helped him enjoy a solid start in life. His ancestors had risen to the level of a royal consort family at one time during the Yi Dynasty, allowing them to prosper, over the years, and become well known and trusted. A daughter of one of his relatives had married into the royal family and Ch'usa was a direct descendant of Kim Han-jin who was a royal son-in-law. This provided Ch'usa some access to power and prestige in eighteenth century Korea.

He was born near the town of Yesan, in South Ch'ungch'ong Province, on 3 June,1786 (lunar calendar). He

After many years of earnest study of classic calligraphy, Kim Chong-hui created and made famous his own style known as *Ch'usach'e*

had the benefit of a good education from an early age and was believed to be a child prodigy. By age six, he was recognized as a promising calligrapher and had reached sufficient sophistication by age fifteen to be accepted as a student by, respected statesman and one time prime minister, Pak Che-ga. The next year, Ch'usa's mother died, while still relatively young, at the age of thirty-four. This was especially traumatic for young Ch'usa as he had experienced the death of two other significant relatives within the span of four years. His uncle, No-yong, who was like a father to him, died when Ch'usa was only twelve. That same year, his grandfather passed away, which was difficult for the young boy to endure. The death of his mother was more painful but was still not the end of his agony. Within five years, his wife, step-mother and aunt all died, which produced significant stress for the young scholar.

In spite of great personal tragedy, he somehow managed to pass the civil service exams at age twenty-three, in 1809. That year would fulfill a dream for Ch'usa that would change his life, for in 1809 his father became vice minister of taxation and was appointed to the Korean delegation to Ching Dynasty China. Ch'usa was allowed to accompany the delegation to the Chinese capital, which afforded Ch'usa the important opportunity to study the Confucian classics in Peking. This was a tremendous opportunity for him and he was reportedly well received there. Ch'usa developed many close relationships, in China, and was able to meet and favorably impress the famous Chinese scholar Weng Fang-gang. Weng became Ch'usa's mentor guiding his studies and exposing him to many ancient masterpieces very few fortunate people are privy to. He also taught him the Chinese classics and introduced Ch'usa to other famous scholars and influential persons. Having become not just an acquaintance, but an actual pupil of the greatest scholars in China at that time, Ch'usa eventually returned to Korea with an advantage unequaled by any scholars in his own country. After returning to Korea, Ch'usa quickly became the leader of the Northern School, a group who imported knowledge of the

West from China. His leadership propelled the effort of historical research and epigraphy in Korea achieving impressive results. He authored a book on ancient inscriptions of Korea, the first of its kind. More historically significant, he established his own style of calligraphy, known as the *ch'usach'e* style. Ch'usa also produced many orchid and landscape style paintings which are still in existence. The Taewongun himself, (see chapter 8) reportedly learned orchid painting from Ch'usa. He labored under many pen names during his life including Yedang, and most commonly, Ch'usa and Wandang. At one point he even became an accomplished Buddhist scholar. He directed historical research on Buddhist philosophy and conducted philosophical discussions with prominent Buddhist scholars, which was not common between Confucian and Buddhist scholars of that period.

Later in life, Ch'usa's family became the object of attack during factional struggles between clans, and while Ch'usa escaped physical harm he was exiled to Cheju Island off the south coast of Korea. He used his time wisely there by continuing his studies and sharing his knowledge with young students on the island. He corresponded frequently with friends and relatives, on the mainland, and received much help and study materials from many of his supporters. It is said that his work became deeper and reached its most advanced state during this period. He was finally freed after nine years in exile, by King Honjong in 1848, but unfortunately for Ch'usa, the king unexpectedly died. Further intrigue in Seoul, after the king's untimely death, brought additional trouble for Ch'usa. Allegations against Ch'usa's objections to the new king, brought him another year in exile in 1851, this time in Pukch'ong, Hamgyong Province. Three years after his return he withdrew to the area of his father's grave in Kwach'on, where he spent the remainder of his years until his death on 10 October, 1856. His birthplace, just north of Yesan has been remodeled and preserved and is open to the public. His grave is also located adjacent to the facility.

He is remembered as a man that raised the level of his

art and made it popular to a larger number of Koreans, enduring great personal tragedy and frustration to continue his craft. He remained focused on his studies but was always willing to share his knowledge with others. He remains a famous character and one of the greatest calligraphers in Korea.

36
Children's Advocate and Political Activist

Pang Chong-hwan
(Sop'a, 1899 -1931)

Individuals contribute to society in many different ways. Some use their abilities to make great breakthroughs in science or medicine, others use their skills to build tall buildings or construct roads and dams, others use their leadership to provide guidance and direction, still others use their imagination to compose stirring music or emotional speeches. Sop'a chose to make his contribution by devoting himself to the future of his country, its children. Although he was an independence fighter he was one of a different sort. He devoted his life to those who had no other advocate. Sop'a wrote many children's stories and started Korea's first children's magazine. He struggled to find toys and places for children to play. Most famous as the founder of Children's Day, his efforts to make children's lives more enjoyable have been recorded and preserved in this national holiday.

Born just before the turn of the century, on 9 November, in Seoul, he was an only child. His father, Pang Kyong-su, tried to provide a good life but young Sop'a endured many hardships in his childhood that later shaped his resolve to promote children's welfare. By the time he was eighteen he

Portrait of Pang Chong-hwan, who devoted himself to the future of his country, its children   BELOW His statue at Children's Grand Park in Seoul

was ready for marriage. He chose Son Yong-hwa, the third daughter of Son Pyong-hui. This was a bit of a coup for Sop'a as the Son family was quite important. Son Pyong-hui was the third head of the Ch'ondogyo Church in Seoul. Ch'ondogyo (Heavenly Way) was started in 1860, and was previously known as Tonghak. When it was disbanded after the Tonghak Rebellion of 1894 it reformed under the name Ch'ondogyo. Son would later help Sop'a publish some of his works but early in Sop'a's marriage, Ch'ondogyo was heavily involved in the independence movement. In fact, Sop'a's father-in-law was one of the original signers of the 1 March, 1919 independence declaration. While all this was unfolding Sop'a was entering Posong College, a two-year professional school (not to be confused with Posong elementary school which Sop'a attended some years before). At the same time Sop'a was helping to publish an independence newspaper in the rear of his home in Seoul. The local police in Chongno suspected his involvement but when they searched his home they found nothing because Sop'a had been clever enough to hide the printing equipment and other incriminating evidence in a nearby well. The police arrested him anyway and interrogated him for one week subjecting him to some severe torture. At one point they hung him upside down and kept pouring water into his nostrils causing painful choking. Another method was to burn his fingers with a hot iron. All this was to no avail as he would not confess and the police allowed him to return home where he quickly returned to publishing the newspaper.

In the spring of 1920, Sop'a traveled to Japan to study children's science at Dongyang College. During a summer vacation in 1922, Sop'a returned to Seoul and started the Seoul chapter of the Ch'ondogyo Youth Association (CYA). The CYA was already active in Chinju, Kwangju and Anbyon (in present day North Korea), and encouraged youth participation in various sports and arts. In that same year, he translated the famous children's book, *Sarangui Sonmul (Love's Gift)* which generated an increased interest in children's literature.

After returning from Japan, Sop'a worked hard to realize his childhood dream. As a child he noticed that many children did not have enough toys or places to play or even books to read. By 1923, Sop'a introduced Korea's first childrens magazine, *Orini*, which means children. In fact, he introduced the word into the Korean language by coining the expression *orini*. The first edition was published on 1 March and the monthly magazine was very successful. In the same year he organized the *Saektonghoe*, a kind of children's issues research group, chartered to improve the welfare of children, which still exists today.

Probably his most memorable achievement was the establishment of Children's Day, which is still a much celebrated national holiday. Sop'a organized the first children's day in an effort to concentrate attention on promoting the health and happiness of Korea's children. Especially during the Japanese colonial period, he felt there was a strong need to improve the life of children and instill a sense of their Korean identity. Because of this nationalistic side of his efforts, the Japanese closely monitored and restricted the development of the holiday. It was originally celebrated on the first of May and continued as such until 1928, when the holiday was changed to the first Sunday in May. Sop'a died on 23 July, 1931 of a heart attack, but the work he started continued. By 1937 however, the Japanese government started restricting certain programs scheduled in conjunction with the holiday and from 1939 until liberation the holiday was prohibited. The first Sunday in May following the liberation, Children's day was again celebrated. This Sunday happened to be 5 May, 1946 and later the holiday was permanently changed to 5 May.

Although he came from a modest family Sop'a rose to prominence through relentless campaigning for children. He has continually been associated with programs and projects that benefit youth. At his tomb in Manguri cemetery, in northeastern Seoul, there is a monument to him. Another statue and memorial to him is appropriately located at the Children's Grand Park in Seoul.

VIII

ARTISTS, WRITERS, PUBLISHERS, COMPOSERS

Ahn Eak-tay

Hong Nanp'a

Kim Song-su

Shin Saimdang

Yi Kwang-su

37
World Renown Musician and Author of the National Anthem

Ahn Eak-tay
(1906-1965)

As an international musical conductor, he may be the best ever produced from Korea. He is a world renown musician and composer in addition to his other musical skills. In fact, he is most famous in Korea as the composer of the Korean national anthem. Ahn left Korea to earn great acclaim in Europe but many Koreans never forgot his contributions to his native land.

At the time of his birth in Pyongyang, in what is now North Korea, the Japanese were already tightening their control over the peninsula. His actual birthday is in question, some sources claiming 1906 and some 1907 or even 1911. By the lunar calendar some Korean sources claim his birthday as 15 December, 1905. He was the third of seven sons born to Ahn Tok-hun. Ahn grew up in a colonized Korea that must have presented serious difficulties for the aspiring musician, who was the son of a simple farmer. Ahn had began studying the violin at nine years old when his older brother gave him a violin as a gift. He learned to play on his own and reportedly had natural talent. In 1918, he attended the Soongsil junior high school in Pyongyang, which was a

Ahn Eak-tay, internationally renowned conductor and composer of the Korean national anthem

Christian missionary school that helped increase his exposure to Western music and instruments. It was at Soongsil that he became interested in the cello and it was his talent with this instrument that brought him recognition as a promising musician. His older brother, who had been away studying in Japan, gave him a cello as a gift while visiting home during summer vacation. These instruments were not common to Korea and were somewhat difficult to obtain. Having his own cello undoubtedly helped the young Ahn to progress more rapidly, but it was difficult to find proper instruction for the cello in Pyongyang. The head of Soongsil spotted the potential talent of the young man and sponsored him to attend formal cello instruction in Seoul. The intense activity in Korea following the 1919 independence movement interrupted Ahn's progress somewhat and his sponsor from Soongsil helped arrange for him to finish school in Japan and live with Ahn's older brother. Ahn finished his studies there and then decided to continue school to broaden his music education.

He enrolled in the Tokyo Music College, to study cello and composition in April 1926 (lunar calendar), and within two months he gave his first concert. He later toured Japan giving solo concerts and earned enough money to pay his school bills. In 1928, his father died, which created some financial problems for Ahn, but with the help of another sponsor he was able to complete his studies. In 1930, he traveled to America with stops in San Francisco and Cincinnati. He earned money along the way with his performances. Later in 1932, he moved to Philadelphia to study at the Curtis Institute of Music. After further study in Philadelphia, he obtained a spot performing, first in the Cincinnati Symphony, and then other orchestras under the direction of some prominent conductors.

At one point, he attended the Royal Academy of Music in Budapest, where he completed a course in music composition. A big break came to him when, in 1936, he moved to Germany and eventually studied under the internationally famous composer Richard Strauss. It was under Strauss's tutelage that he developed his well-known work "Fantasy Korea."

The story of how the Korean National Anthem was actually composed is not completely clear but Ahn is said to have worked on the music for a number of years, listening to scores of national anthems from many other countries and researching the background of their music. The actual lyrics to the present Korean national anthem, *Aegukka*, are believed to have been the result of a collaboration of many authors and are not attributed to a single individual. After finishing the music, Ahn sent it to a Korean church in San Francisco which promoted it and eventually forwarded it to the Korean government-in-exile, in Shanghai. It made its debut, in 1938, with the Irish National Symphony and was inserted into programs around the globe as Ahn toured the world conducting various orchestras. The song had become dear to Koreans late in the Japanese colonial period and was finally adopted as the national anthem by, the newly formed, Republic of Korea in 1948.

In the meantime Ahn's fame had continued to build. He had moved to Spain in 1944 and became a frequent conductor of the Barcelona Symphony. He had been a guest conductor for orchestras in many cities of the world, such as Rome, London, Tokyo, Manila, Budapest, and other cities in Brazil, Switzerland and the United States, to name a few. He married the daughter of a Spanish count, made his home in Mallorca Spain, and eventually had three daughters.

He returned to Korea in 1955, for the first time in twenty-five years, to perform for the celebration of President Rhee Syng-man's 80th birthday. He returned several more times before he died in a Barcelona hospital from a liver ailment on 17 September, 1965. Initially, he was buried in Spain but after much effort his remains were returned to his homeland in July 1977. He is buried at the National Cemetery in Seoul in a plot especially designated for meritorious citizens.

As the Francis Scott Key of Korea, he is known by most Koreans as the composer of the national anthem. Many others however, remember him for the emotions he stirred with the music he wrote during an emotional period of Korea's colonial years. Still others appreciate the recognition he brought, not just to himself, but to Korea as one of the first internationally recognized Korean musicians respected in the West.

38
Patriotic Composer and Violinist
Hong Nanp'a
(1897-1941)

A brilliant composer and violinist, Nanp'a, as he is known, was also a writer of short stories and children's songs. Most of his works were Western style music with Korean lyrics and he is often credited with helping introduce Western music to Korea. His extraordinary songs however, touched the hearts of Koreans everywhere during the painful and difficult Japanese colonial period.

He was born with the name Hong Yong-hu, on 10 April, in Hwasong-gun, Kyonggi Province. They were a simple farming family with four sons and two daughters; Nanp'a was the second son. Later in 1898, the family moved to Seoul to live with the oldest son, Hong Sok-hu, Nanp'a's older brother. This brother, who was fifteen years older than Nanp'a, provided important assistance to the entire Hong family. He had started school at the YMCA in Seoul and later went to America to finish his studies in medicine. He returned to Korea to become a successful eye doctor and the income he earned helped the entire family, especially Nanp'a.

While attending school, Nanp'a met a teacher, Kim In-

Hong Nanp'a, who touched the hearts of Koreans with his stirring music during the Japanese colonial period

shik, who in 1910, encouraged him to take up the violin. At that time not many people were familiar with the violin and Koreans didn't even call it as such, they called it a *yang kkangkkang*; which humorously enough, roughly translates as *yang* meaning Western, and *kkangkkang* being the sound it makes when you play it. Kim provided the violin and Nanp'a practiced diligently carrying the instrument home with him everyday. The sight of the boy carrying the strange case through the streets aroused the suspicion of the local police who stopped and questioned him many times about what was inside.

In 1914, Nanp'a entered a music school (Choson Chongak Chonsupso), and after he graduated he stayed on as a young teacher. NanP'a wanted to continue studying music but his parents were upset with his choice of vocations. They preferred a more honorable course for their son, similar to that of his older brother, and after strong persuasion Nanp'a entered Severance Medical School. His mind was always with music not medicine, however, and he quickly fell behind in his studies which he had paid relatively little attention to. Within a few years his brother helped sponsor his travel to Japan to continue his music studies. He studied in Tokyo at the Ueno Music School which he enjoyed but his life would be interrupted by political events at home. The independence movement was growing in Korea and among students in Japan. Just before the March 1919 movement, Nanp'a became involved in disseminating anti-Japanese literature among students in Tokyo. Following the subsequent Japanese crackdown, Nanp'a's activities were identified and he returned to Korea to temporarily escape danger. His involvement in the independence movement turned into encouragement for the movement through what he did best—music. He wrote songs that stirred the emotions of Koreans and uplifted their spirits. His first was in April 1920 when he wrote "Pongsonwha" (Touch-me-not Flower) which is still famous today. This song was one of his most famous and helped him gain popularity, as it was reportedly known as the song of the resistance movement. Within a short while he was back teaching music again and perfecting his own ability. In 1924, he gave the first solo violin performance in Korea and in September the following year he gave his first concert at the YMCA in Seoul. After a stint teaching at the Chungang Music School he traveled to America to study for a while at the Sherwood Music School in Chicago in 1931. He came back to Seoul ready to tour again and continue his work.

1934 was an important year for Nanp'a as he started teaching at Ewha Womans University and by the end of the year (27 December), married Yi T'ae-yong. They bought a house in Chong-dong, Seoul and Nanp'a continued teaching. He eventually became vice-president of Kyongsong Broadcasting System which was the forerunner of today's Korea Broadcasting System. Nanp'a founded Kyongsong's philharmonic orchestra in 1936 and continued to rise in popularity. His many songs continued to provide comfort to the people and stir their national pride. The following year, however, he became involved in Hungsadan, a group established to help encourage nationalism and cooperation among Koreans. This brought him under closer scrutiny of the police, ever watchful for dissidents and opposition to the colonial government. He was called in for questioning and spent three months in prison. Many other nationalists, who had been educated in America, were also questioned and put on notice that their activities would be closely followed. The three months in prison were not easy. Inmates could rarely bathe and were fed a kind of gruel in addition to the difficult and painful interrogations. When his wife finally came to bring him home, on his release day, she could barely recognize him. The clothes he wore were tattered and filthy and his smell and appearance were saddening.

Even though only in prison a short while, he was never the same again. The authorities would call him at least once a month to keep track of the family's activities and maintain pressure on them. He finally developed pleurisy and was soon too sick to earn much income. They were forced to sell one of his most prized possessions, his piano, to raise money in 1940. Nanp'a promised his wife he would buy it back when he regained his health, but was never able to as he died the following year on 30 August. His last request was to be cremated with his conductor attire next to him. His early death left his wife and two daughters behind.

Danguk University in Seoul maintains a small museum, at the memorial hall named for him, with some of Nanp'a's possessions on display there. There is also a statue commemorating him at the KBS studios on Youido in Seoul and his birthplace is a historical site. His contributions to Korean music and the independence movement are well remembered and appreciated.

39
Noted Publisher and Financier

Kim Song-su
(Inch'on, 1891-1955)

Businessman, politician, publisher and independence fighter, Kim worked hard to help others and used his talents and money, to sponsor many activities and establishments to help those less fortunate. Although he would eventually reach high government office in the Rhee administration, he was mostly known as someone who worked better behind the scenes, organizing and creating an atmosphere of cooperation that produced progress. He may be best known as one of the founders of the *Dong-A Ilbo* (a highly respected newspaper), and a benefactor of, present day, Korea University. His many accomplishments make him well known throughout Korea.

Born in Koch'ang-gun, North Cholla Province, on 11 October, Kim was fortunate to have a family with some wealth and a respected ancestry. The Kim family had made their money mostly in real estate, even as the Japanese were tightening their grip on the country. Adopted by his father's older brother, Kim Ki-jung, in 1893, Kim would grow up somewhat privileged. He did not squander his wealth however, but compounded it through shrewd investment and

Early photo of Kim Song-su before his success as a businessman, newspaper publisher and founder of Korea University

business opportunity. He married in 1903, at an early age even by Korean custom, and in 1910 his first son, Kim Sangman, was born. That same year, Kim moved to Japan to attend Waseda University, returning to Seoul four years later, after graduation.

In 1919, he established the Kyongsong Textile Company which was a purely Korean company, began with purely Korean funds, and which took great pride in hiring only Korean employees. This company, with the nationalist tint, caught on and its products were probably bought as much for patriotism as for quality.

At the relatively early age of twenty-nine, he helped found the *Dong-A* daily newspaper, which although it experienced some censorship and other punitive actions under the Japanese, has grown into one of the nation's largest and most respected newspapers. Kim used the newspaper as his means to contribute to the independence movement by enlightening the people and helping keep nationalism alive during the Japanese colonial period. His efforts and criticism of the Japanese, caused the newspaper along with the *Chosun Ilbo,* another popular newspaper, to be shut down four separate times during the years 1926 through 1940. Both papers were suspended indefinitely in 1940, and did not resume publishing until after the end of World War II.

Firmly believing that Korea's future depended on an educated and developed nation, Kim sponsored various educational establishments. He took control of Posong College in 1932, when the school was in serious financial difficulty. About a year later, he purchased a large plot of land in Anam-dong, in northeastern Seoul, and hired a Korean architect to create a new image for the school. After consulting with the architect Kim decided to model the design of the main building after that of Duke University in North Carolina. The new building was finally dedicated and the campus moved to Anam-dong in 1934. After liberation, the university's name was changed to Korea University. With Kim's substantial assistance it has grown to one of the leading universities in Korea.

After liberation, Kim helped finance and organize the Korea Democratic Party (KDP), in September 1945, in an attempt to unite various right wing groups in opposition to a significant socialist and communist party presence growing in the South. The KDP was a major influence in the political process and the formation of the Republic of Korea in 1948. The KDP gave significant support to Rhee Syng-man and was a major factor in his rise to the top political post. When Rhee was elected president in 1948, Kim expected to receive a top post in the administration but was only offered the job of Finance Minister. Rhee was criticized as not having any opposition members in key positions in his administration. Many had expected him to form a coalition government bringing together some of the key figures from various parties, including men like Kim Song-su and Kim Koo. This did not fit Rhee's political game plan which relied on strong central control with him at the helm. Rhee's administration had many political difficulties because of this. In April 1951, Vice President Yi Shi-yong resigned in protest after a scandal within the administration. Strong pressure was applied to have Kim take the position, which he did, only to resign himself in May the following year in protest over the arrest of some anti-Rhee legislators.

Not long after, Kim became ill and in the following years his health deteriorated slowly until his eventual death in 1955. He had spent a lifetime trying to harmonize people and direct their efforts toward productive progress.

A large statue of Kim still stands on campus at Korea University, in front of the administration building and a beautiful auditorium is named for him there. There is also a museum on campus that maintains a few articles pertaining to him. His grave was also located on campus at one time but was moved to Masok in December 1987. In addition, Kim's house, and one time memorial, has been remodeled and restored in Kye-dong, Chongno-gu, Seoul, but it is not open to the public. It is kept by the *Dong-A Ilbo* newspaper for private functions and contains a statue of Kim and his father in the garden.

40
Respected Artist and Quintessential Mother

Shin Saimdang
(1504 -1551)

Certainly of the Yi Dynasty (1392-1910), if not the entire history of Korea, Shin Saimdang is the most respected and remembered woman in Korea. She is revered as the quintessential mother, wife and daughter. Her artistic talents are well-known in the fields of painting, calligraphy, embroidery and poetry. She is often referred to as the mother of Yi Yi (Yulgok, see chapter 23). Unfortunately, while her famous philosopher son sometimes overshadows her, Shin Saimdang's individual talents made her a woman to emulate and earned her a permanent place in Korean history.

The little village of Pukp'yong, now within the city of Kangnung, on the east coast of Korea, was her birthplace. She was born there on 29 October (lunar calendar) in the tenth year of King Yonsan's reign. Yonsan was a hated king and was soon deposed and replaced by King Chungjong who was a much more benevolent ruler. She lived most of her life during the reign of this famous monarch.

Shin Saimdang's father, Shin Myong-hwa had an aristocratic heritage. Shin Saimdang was the second of five daughters. She had no brothers. Her real name was Shin Yi-son.

Shin Saimdang, quintessential mother of Korea. She is also remembered as an accomplished artist and poet

She took the pen name Saimdang (pronounced Sa-Im-Dang) from a famous Korean story about the mother of the Chinese King Mun. The king's mother's name was Taim, and she was known for her integrity and keen wit. The name, Saimdang, was created from part of the queen's name and means, roughly translated, respect to Queen Mother Taim.

Saimdang's parents saw to her education at an early age and she displayed unusual talents in the arts almost from the beginning. She was also schooled in the Confucian classics and was especially interested in Confucian philosophy.

At the age of nineteen, she married Yi Won-su, then twenty-two, who was a distant relative of the famous naval hero Admiral Yi Sun-shin. Yi Won-su went on to become a scholar and government official, although he progressed somewhat slowly and never achieved very high office.

In the same year she married, her father died and Saimdang mourned for the traditional three years. She later went to live with her husband's family in the village of Yulgok which means, Chestnut Valley, and is the name her famous son later took as his pen name. She could not stay there permanently however, because her mother was still living alone near Kangnung. Saimdang traveled as much as possible between the two locations to look after her mother. This was extremely difficult as both places were in the countryside and somewhat difficult to reach. Saimdang persisted however, out of devotion to her mother and in fulfillment of her obligations as a daughter.

Saimdang had seven children, four sons and three daughters. Her son Yulgok was the third and was born when she was thirty-two years old. She personally saw to Yulgok's education in the Confucian classics and Yulgok advanced rapidly. Under her supervision he had mastered the classics by the age of seven and was writing poetry by the age of eight. Yulgok continued to excel into his teens. Sometime around 1551, Saimdang's husband obtained a position as a tax official and was forced to travel to P'yongan Province. He took Yulgok and Yulgok's brother with him. While they were away Saimdang became very ill and died before her husband

and two sons could return. She was only forty-seven at her death and her young son Yulgok was only fifteen. Her husband died some ten years later in 1561.

She is buried in P'aju-gun, which is in Kyonggi Province. Her tomb is in pleasant surroundings next to her husband and just below her famous son Yulgok.

Although she is a celebrated poet only two of her poems exist today in their entirety. Both of these famous poems refer to her mother who was apparently constantly in her thoughts. Some portions of her other poetry exist but are sometimes difficult to fully grasp without the complete text. She is also noted for her calligraphy but, unfortunately, only seven pieces of her work can still be found. Her paintings too are treasures of Korea. She is said to have begun painting by copying the works of the renowned artist Ahn Kyon. She started painting at the age of seven and developed great skill at various styles. Her landscape paintings are probably her most famous today and are ranked by some in the category with the great artist she first loved to copy. A statue honoring her stands at Sajik Park in downtown Seoul, and a street in downtown Seoul, Saimdang-ro, is named after her. Her shrine is located at Ojuk'on, in Kangnung. This shrine contains her official portrait and many of her paintings and calligraphy. Her birthplace and the house she lived in are attached to the shrine. Many items relating to her son, are also located there as the facility doubles as a shrine to Yulgok who was also born there and spent his youth learning from his mother in the same house. Just a few kilometers away, at Kyongp'odae, is a large bronze statue of Saimdang seated reading her calligraphy.

Although not much has been written about her in English her story is celebrated among Koreans as a woman to truly emulate. Her devotion to family, in addition to her individual talents, are legendary.

41
Novelist and Literary Genius

Yi Kwang-su
(Ch'unwon, 1892 –1950)

The many facets of this extraordinary man include, writer, poet, journalist, teacher, political activist and independence fighter. Yi Kwang-su was both loved and hated by his countrymen. Some would call him patriot, some have called him traitor. Many have not fully understood his life. Most assuredly, however, he played a role in the Korean independence movement and has touched the thoughts of many with his various novels and journalistic pieces.

The year of 1892 was a year of transition to turmoil in Korea. The Tonghak movement was stirring up dissent in the southern provinces. The Tonghak (Eastern Learning) was opposed to subservience to China while simultaneously criticizing Western learning and Catholicism. Within two years they would be in full revolt but, in 1892, the year Yi was born, they were still in preparation. Yi was born in North P'yongan Province, in what is now North Korea. Although his family was not rich they were of the *yangban* or aristocratic class. Yi's education was traditionally Confucian. He was tutored at an early age in the Confucian classics, at which he excelled.

Yi Kwang-su, distinguished writer and controversial patriot

When Yi was approximately nine years old his father died during a cholera epidemic and his mother died a few weeks later. His baby sister died about a year later from dysentery. Things looked rather bleak for the young lad until Yi was given a job as a messenger for the regional commander of the Tonghak movement. Yi was only ten years old at the time. By 1904, the threat of war between Japan and Russia was menacing Korea. The Japanese had strengthened their hold on Korea after winning the Sino-Japanese war of 1894-95. The Japanese were concerned about agitation from the Tonghak and started making preemptive arrests in 1904. Yi fled to Seoul where he was fortunate enough to receive a scholarship to study in Japan. The scholarship was funded by Ch'ondogyo which was the reformed Tonghak organization after the Japanese shut it down in 1904 for its political activities. Of course Japan did go to war with Russia in 1904 and had defeated them by 1905. Having eliminated their major rivals for control of the peninsula, Japan annexed Korea in 1910.

Yi completed his high school education in Japan and then traveled some in China and Russia before enrolling in Waseda University in 1915. It was during these college years (1917), that he published his first novel, *The Heartless (Mujong)*, which was very successful. It was also during this period Yi discovered he had contracted tuberculosis.

Yi's former Ch'ondogyo friends informed him of the impending independece movement and asked Yi to draft a declaration of independence from Japan and help distribute it in Tokyo. On 1 March, 1919, the declaration was read and the independence movement began. The Japanese quickly retaliated with arrests, torture and floggings. Expecting arrest, as the author of the declaration, Yi left for Shanghai two weeks earlier. There he helped other independence fighters establish a provisional government in exile. Strangely enough when Yi returned to Korea in 1921 the Japanese arrested him for a short period and then released him, which gave some Koreans the impression he may have been a collaborator. Yi continued to write essays and was given a job as an editorial writer for the *Dong-A Ilbo* newspaper in Seoul. In 1924, Yi secretly traveled to China to meet independence leader Ahn Ch'ang-ho (see chapter 42) and deliver his messages to the people through the *Dong-A Ilbo*. He continued his activities until 1933 when he left the *Dong-A Ilbo* to become vice president of the *Chosun Ilbo* daily newspaper. Yi was imprisoned by the Japanese in 1937 because of his activities but released within six months because of serious health problems. He began writing some of his best novels shortly after. Yi made the decision to submit to some of the Japanese demands as their methods of persuasion became even more harsh during World War II. He even wrote some pro-Japanese essays to preclude Japanese mistreatment.

After the war, he settled close to Seoul and taught at a junior high school. He also used this time to continue writing and completed a biography of Ahn Ch'ang-ho. The new Korean government established a special committee to investigate alleged Japanese collaborators. They arrested Yi and later cleared and released him in 1949. When the Korean War erupted in 1950, Yi was abducted to the North and never heard from again. Only recently was it confirmed that he died in December 1950 at a military hospital in North P'yongan Province in North Korea.

This fascinating man who had done so much for his country and made so much of early troubled circumstances, became very controversial in the later part of his life. As some argue Yi's motives none can deny his contributions in poetry, literature and politics. Some of his other famous novels include *The Soil, The Twilight,* and *Unenlightened.*

IX

PATRIOTS
(Independence Fighters)

Ahn Ch'ang-ho

Ahn Chung-gun

Kim Koo

Kim Ok-kyun

Shin Ch'ae-ho

So Chae-p'il

Yi Sang-jae

Yu Kwan-sun

Yun Pong-gil

42
Inspiring Orator

Ahn Ch'ang-ho
(Tosan, 1878 -1939)

One of Korea's most respected independence fighters, Ahn was a soft spoken but powerful orator who helped forge the Korean independence movement during the Japanese colonial period. He was a politician but some say, even more, he was an educator. One thing for certain, Ahn had a vision of Korea that included modernization and independence and he struggled to help Korea fulfill that vision with all his energy.

Ahn was born in what is now North Korea, in a small outlying village of Pyongyang, on 9 November 1878 (lunar calendar). His beginnings were of a simple farming family. As did many children of the Yi Dynasty, Ahn's education began with the Chinese classics. He studied so for eight years beginning when he was seven. He then enrolled in a Western style school run by the Salvation Army and graduated at the age of eighteen. He witnessed parts of the Sino-Japanese War (1894-95) which occurred while he was in school. Seeing the two countries struggling for control of his country, on the very soil of Korea, caused Ahn to realize how weak Korea was at that period. He decided that Korea

Ahn Ch'ang-ho, sincere patriot who believed that true independence was accomplished through education

would require tremendous change if it were ever to become strong enough to maintain its autonomy in the midst of the great powers surrounding the tiny country. Ahn became committed to Korean modernization and independence.

Soon after the war, in 1896, other independence-minded Koreans established the Independence Club (Tongnip Hyop'oe). Many famous reformers like So Chae-p'il and Rhee Syng-man, were active in the club. Ahn joined a year later and soon organized a chapter in Pyongyang. Convinced that one certain prerequisite to modernization was education, Ahn established a primary school in his hometown. He continued his efforts into the new century when he married and decided to travel to the United States. Arriving in San Francisco in 1902, he was soon disappointed by the lives of Koreans living there. He devoted himself to improving their lot and soon won the admiration of the Korean community there.

Although he was in the U.S. during the Russo-Japanese War (1904-5), Ahn returned to Korea in 1906 to energize the independence spirit among Koreans even as Japan tightened its grip more firmly on the country. He toured Korea, lecturing, organizing and teaching. He established a ceramics company in the southern city of Masan to help raise money for the movement and he established a school in Pyongyang called Taesong, to influence the minds of young people. Just when the annexation of Korea was proceeding in 1910, he made a second trip to the United States by way of Russia and Europe, actually arriving in 1911. He tried establishing Korean groups in the U.S. but was never truly successful with the exception of Hungsadan. This group was formed in the U.S., in 1913, to promote Korean independence and train leaders to help achieve it. Incredibly, the organization still exists today as a caretaker of Ahn's writings and thoughts.

A few years after forming Hungsadan, the Korean independence movement burst into action on 1 March, 1919. Ahn, almost immediately fled to China and helped form the provisional government in Shanghai. He was appointed Premier and held that post until 1921. He continued with his anti-Japanese activities among Koreans in Manchuria and was actually arrested and released by the Japanese in 1927. Finally, however, he was arrested in Shanghai after the Yun Pong-gil (see chapter 50) bombing incident there, in 1932, killed some top Japanese officials. Actually, Ahn was not involved but served four years in prison, in the Korean city of Taejon, for the offense. After his release he traveled the country, speaking, but the Japanese restricted him in many ways. Police arrested Ahn again about one month before the start of the next Sino-Japanese War (1937-45). He was later released and allowed to receive treatment for stomach and liver problems at Seoul National University Hospital. He died there on 10 March, 1938.

Ahn was often known by his pen name, Tosan, which means mountain of knowledge. He is buried on the south side of Seoul with his wife, in Tosan Park. The park, located in Apkujong-dong, also contains a large bronze statue of him. Incidentally, the grounds are a frequent site for newly-weds who often have their pictures taken in the pleasant surroundings. At the Independence Hall in Ch'onan, some of his personal belongings are exhibited and there are many other displays relating to him.

Ahn fathered five children, all born in the U.S., who have gone on to successful lives. He is sometimes called Korea's number one patriot. For certain, he will long be remembered as a major figure during Korea's struggle to break the Japanese colonial grip in the early twentieth century and restore Korean independence.

43
Man of Patriotic Action

Ahn Chung-gun
(1879-1910)

His is a name known well to Koreans and most always preceded by the word patriot. He is not known for his dynamic oratory or historic compositions, etc., but for his efforts as an independence fighter. His distinguished role in the anti-Japanese struggle was the assassination of Japanese statesman Itō Hirobumi in 1909. This courageous act eventually cost him his life but was an inspiration to Koreans all over the world throughout the Japanese occupation and the subsequent independence movement.

Not much is recorded about the early life of Ahn. He was born during the period of Korea's opening to foreigners and grew up as Japan was systematically moving to control the peninsula. His hometown is Haeju, Hwanghae Province, where he spent much of his youth in the mountains nearby. In 1905, he moved to Chinnamp'o and founded a school where he taught for a few years. Ahn had married young, to Kim A-ryo, and had begun a family of his own early.

He had become an admirer of another famous Ahn, Ahn Ch'ang-ho, and was very interested in his thoughts on Korean independence. Sometime around 1907 he left his

Photo of Ahn Chung-gun shortly after his assassination of Itō Hirobumi in 1909

Ahn, among his captors, meeting with some family members just before his execution in 1910

family and traveled to Manchuria where he helped organize other Koreans in the Korean Volunteer Army which disrupted Japanese operations in the region. While in Manchuria, he heard of the upcoming visit of Ito Hirobumi to Harbin and resolved to assassinate him.

Ito had been named the first Resident General of Korea in 1905 after the Japanese defeated the Russians in the Russo-Japanese War (1904-5). The Treaty of Portsmouth, which negotiated the end of the war, gave Japan virtual control over Manchuria and all of Korea's foreign relations. Japan moved quickly to control its new possessions by installing commissioners in Seoul and one in every province throughout the country. After Ito arrived in Seoul all foreign legations were soon withdrawn. After the abdication of King Kojong in 1907, Itō helped conclude an agreement that even further strengthened, Japan's control of Korea. On the same day of the agreement a press law was instituted which banned all nationalistic books and restricted or closed some newspapers. Within a week, the Korean Army was also disbanded and the Japanese assumed control of the police and judicial systems. For these and other reasons Itō is often labeled as the engineer of Japan's takeover of Korea. He had become a symbol of colonialism Koreans could focus their hatred on. Itō later became the chairman of a group that advised the Japanese emperor on territorial expansion. As part of his duties, he planned to travel to Harbin to meet with the Russian Minister of Finance and inspect northern Manchuria in October of 1909. Itō left on the inspection tour and arrived in Harbin at around 9:00 a.m. on 26 October.

By disguising himself as a Japanese reporter, Ahn was able to obtain access very close to the arriving dignitaries. Almost as soon as Itō arrived he proceeded to inspect some Russian Army troops at the train station, who had turned out for the occasion. At that moment, Ahn burst from the crowd and shot Itō three times, once each in the chest, stomach and shoulder. Additional shots missed Itō but hit other Japanese dignitaries traveling with the party. Ahn was quickly arrested by the Russian military police. Itō died fairly quickly thereafter and Ahn was taken to a prison in Manchuria.

Throughout his captivity, Ahn insisted he be treated not as a criminal but as a prisoner of war. He argued that he was leading Korean troops against the Japanese at the time and killed Itō as an act of war. The Japanese, of course, did not agree. He was sentenced and later executed on 26 March, 1910 in Lushin Prison in China, at the age of thirty-one. Less than five months later Japan officially annexed Korea.

Still today, Ahn is one of the most celebrated and remembered of Korea's independence fighters. A museum honoring him is located in the park on Namsan mountain in the center of the capital. There is also a large statue and outdoor memorial located there. Additional displays and a statue honoring him are located at the Independence Hall in Ch'onan. A few photos and some other memorabilia of Ahn's can be seen at the Choltusan Shrine, in Map'o, in western Seoul.

This young man continues to be remembered by Koreans as one who committed the ultimate sacrifice for a greater cause during a time of great physical and emotional hardship for Korea. Although his act had no real affect on Japan's eventual annexation of the country, it did provide some inspiration and hope that Koreans had not capitulated to Japan's efforts to absorb the country. It may also have provided some courage to those who, throughout the Japanese occupation, continued to resist the Japanese through the independence movement.

44
Enduring Patriot

Kim Koo
(Paekpom, 1876-1949)

Kim Koo is one of the most famous of Korea's national independence fighters. He is most noted for involvement in the 1 March, 1919 independence movement, his role in the creation of the provisional government in Shanghai China during the Japanese occupation of Korea, and his anti-Japanese activities during that period. He is also well remembered for his autobiography, written under the penname Paekpom, which has become a classic.

Kim Koo was born on 11 July, 1876 (lunar calendar) in Haeju, Hwanghae Province, in what is now part of North Korea. He was of humble origin, the only son of Kim Sunyong. Even though his family was not of wealth, his parents were particular to ensure Kim received a proper education. He struggled to master the basic Chinese characters and studied hard to prepare for the government examinations. When he failed his exams he blamed the corrupt system that allowed others to bribe their way through the exams. He grew up during the last decades of the Yi Dynasty and was deeply influenced and disillusioned by the apparent corruption of those times. Kim joined the Tonghak (Eastern

Photo of Kim Koo, one of the most famous of Korea's national independence fighters and statesman

Kim at the 38th parallel just before crossing into North Korea in 1948 to attempt reconciliation between South and North Korea. Kim Shin, his son, to his right

Learning) movement which was a religious movement spreading among farmers of Korea in the late 1800's. During the Tonghak Rebellion of 1894, Kim was active and reportedly led some 700 followers against the Haeju castle but was driven back by Japanese troops.

The last years of the nineteenth century were turbulent times for Korea. In August 1896 Queen Min, wife of King Kojong, was killed by Japanese troops in Seoul. Although in Manchuria at the time, Kim avenged the queen's death by returning and killing a Japanese army officer. He was arrested and served time in prison in Inch'on until his escape about a year later. In 1909, he was again imprisoned for his involvement in the assassination of Ito Hirobumi, by Ahn Chung-gun (see chapter 43). After five years in prison he was released and spent the next few years roaming Korea conducting anti-Japanese activity as part of the Shinminhoe, an organization formed to help enlighten Koreans about Japan's colonization of Korea.

In 1919, as part of the independence movement, he traveled to Shanghai China to help create a provisional government in exile there. Kim became the leader of that body in 1927. Under the leadership of Kim this government played a critical role in anti-Japanese activities by Koreans. Kim also formed the Korean Independence Party and was chosen as the chairman of its executive council. In 1935, Kim organized a new political party known as the Korean People's Party due to a struggle between right and left wing political factions. He later established an army to aid the allies in their efforts against the Japanese during World War II. This army became known as the Kwangbok (Liberation) Army. Kim worked tirelessly to influence Korea's post-war development. He is believed to have asked Chiang Kai-shek to include a statement concerning Korea in allied negotiations which is believed to have resulted in the famous statement concerning Korea's future independence which was part of the famous Cairo Declaration. The declaration was the result of a conference held in Cairo, in 1943, between President Franklin Roosevelt, Prime Minister Winston Churchill and General

Chiang. Following World War II, Kim returned to Korea and opposed efforts to divide the Korean peninsula. Kim's ideas of government and methods to maintain unity on the Korean peninsula clashed with those of another important independence fighter, Rhee Syng-man. Kim sought compromise with North Korea and traveled there with Kim Kyu-shik to meet North Korean leader Kim Il-sung on 19 April, 1948. The talks were labeled a failure and Kim returned to Seoul still intent on boycotting the United Nations sponsored elections. His battle for control of the South Korean government and his feud with Rhee continued but to no avail. Rhee prevailed and was elected president in May 1948.

On 26 June, 1948, Kim was assassinated by an army second lieutenant Ahn Tu-hui who shot Kim twice in the head and twice in the stomach. The incident took place at a house in Seoul where Kim was residing at the time. Some speculated the assassination may have been connected to the political problems associated with the forming of the South Korean government in 1948. In April 1992, Kim's assassin came forth with information confirming government involvement in Kim's death.

Kim was buried in Hyoch'ang Park in west-central Seoul. The Association of Commemorative Services for Kim Koo is located nearby in Hyoch'ang-dong. They have an extensive library and some displays relating to him there. There are many historical documents and materials relating to Kim at the Independence Hall near Ch'onan. The museum also boasts a life-size wax figure of him in the hall relating to the provisional government. There is also a large statue and memorial to Kim located on Namsan Mountain, in central Seoul, situated in the park, Paekpom Plaza, named for him.

45
Daring Government Reformer

Kim Ok-kyun
(1851-1894)

On the vanguard of the reform movement of the late nineteenth century, Kim was instrumental in the Kapshin Coup of 1884. Although the effort was unsuccessful it triggered events that permanently changed the political face of the entire country.

Pioneer is the word often used to describe this reformer. Kim worked himself into a position that gave him frequent access to King Kojong and, in his case, access meant influence. This was a significant accomplishment considering he was not born of a wealthy or notable family.

Born as the first son of Kim Pyong-t'ae on 23 February, 1851, not much is known about his early life. He was from Ch'ungch'ong Province but which city is still a mystery. His mother and father appear to have been simple people. His father did not hold any high government office and did not own any land. At some point his parents allowed Kim to be adopted by a more wealthy member of the same clan. Kim Pyong-gi became Kim's new father. He was related to Kim Pyong-t'ae by a common great grandfather. This new family must have worked well for Kim because by the time he

213

Kim Ok-kyun, clearly ahead of his time, this man of vision ultimately failed in his attempt to reform the government of 19th century Korea

reached twenty-one he passed the higher civil service exam with highest honors. Over the next ten years, until he left for Japan in 1882, Kim held various lower level posts in a part of government similar to what some would call an Inspector Generals office. According to official records, Kim advanced slowly and his promotions were unimpressive. However, his position, and the fact that he had begun work rather early in life, gave him frequent and extensive contact with the king.

In the eighteenth and nineteenth century the reform movement known as *Shirhak* or practical learning blossomed. Korea was having serious internal problems with government irregularities and internal rebellion. In the nineteenth century Korea was also receiving considerable outside pressure to open up to foreigners. There was great division within Korea on how to tackle these nagging difficulties. In addition, China still maintained considerable influence and control over many aspects of Korean politics. *Shirhak* advocated reform of government institutions, construction of better roads, efficient utilization of natural resources, promotion of education and various other improvements to society. *Shirhak* proposed that government policies be constructed based on their utility and ability to improve the welfare of the people. Kim became acquainted with this movement early in his professional life. He became friends with a government official who was also interested in *Shirhak*. Kim quickly made friends with others interested in modernization of Korea. In 1881, two of Kim's friends were part of group of Koreans King Kojong sent to Japan to report on Japan's modernization. Kim learned much from his friends upon their return and the group's report also influenced the king. It is believed that Kim made a conscious decision to devote his efforts to modernization of Korea even at the expense of his own advancement in the government.

In February of 1882, Kim was allowed to make his own trip to Japan to learn first-hand about modernization in that country. This was the first of three trips in two years for Kim. By his third trip he had impressed the king enough that he was sent to Japan with a title and some authority to act on behalf of the government. The stage was set for the 1884 incident. Kim had advanced enough in those two years to put him in a position to effect some change in the government. He had made many friends in Japan and was determined to expedite Korea's progress and reform.

On 4 December, 1884, Kim and some of his close companions, staged a bloody coup to try and form a new government. This incident known as the Kapshin Coup was initially successful. Kim was able to form an administration and proclaim a new government. They formed this government under Japanese military protection. A small band of Japanese soldiers from the legation helped provide security. Within a few days the Chinese moved to suppress the coup. After a brief skirmish, the Japanese protectors retreated to their legation and Kim and some of the other reformers were forced to flee to Japan.

The coup failed and Kim never returned to Korea again. He spent most of the next ten years in various locations within Japan. He was finally assassinated on 28 March, 1894 in Shanghai China. The incident he spearheaded precipitated more animosity in the Sino-Japanese rivalry over Korea which eventually led to the Sino-Japanese War (1894-95) and the ultimate annexation of Korea by Japan in 1910.

46
Honored Historian

Shin Ch'ae-ho
(Tanjae, 1880 -1936)

It is hard to determine if Tanjae is more famous as an historian or an independence fighter. Through his life he redefined modern Korean history and used his writing to foster and encourage nationalism. In the end, the fight for independence, during the Japanese colonial period, cost him his life. He died for independence but he lived to awaken the common people of Korea to the importance and richness of their past. This famous historian and independence figure played an influential role in the development of Korea from the turn of the twentieth century.

West of Taejon, in Taedok, South Ch'ungch'ong Province, Tanjae was born on 7 November, 1880. His family were simple farmers but they had a proud ancestry of Yi Dynasty scholars and government officials. The unfortunate death of his father when Tanjae was only seven left his family in an even more difficult situation. The matter of young Tanjae's education fell upon his grandfather who tutored him in the traditional classics until Tanjae reached eighteen. From a relatively early age he showed an ability in education with a special gift for writing. Even though they were poor

Shin Ch'ae-ho, who successfully instilled pride in Koreans through his colorful descriptions of famous historical Korean heroes

Tanjae's family wanted the best education for him. In the late nineteenth century, one of the most famous and prestigious universities in Korea was Sunggyungwan. This institution has a history dating back to the fourth century. Shortly after the start of the Yi Dynasty, in 1392, however, the university began evolving into an important producer of scholars for the Confucian-based dynasty. It was at its best in the late nineteenth century when Tanjae enrolled in the fall of 1898.

Although he was only eighteen when he entered college, he already had a sincere interest in Korea's future development. It was fairly clear that Korea was being slowly engulfed by Japan. Fear that Korea would someday lose its autonomy involved him in a patriotic movement to instill nationalism in the populace. He became a young activist and joined the famous Independence Club in the same year he enrolled in college. By 1905, he became a *paksa*, or Ph.D., at the university and the editorial writer for the *Hwangsong Shinmun (Hwangsong Daily Newspaper)*. In the following year he took a key position as the chief editor of the *Daehan Maeil Shinmun (Korean Daily Newspaper)*. From this position he had the ability and the inclination to influence Koreans and imbue their thoughts with nationalism.

By resurrecting the colorful histories of respected leaders of the past he hoped to renew a pride and patriotic spirit to compensate for the Japanese attempts to dissolve the Korean identity. He wrote and published various important works beginning with the *Biography of Admiral Yi Sun-shin (Yi Ch'ungmugong Chon)*, *Biography of General Ulchi Mundok (Ulchi Mundok Chon)*, and *A History of Ancient Korea (Choson Sanggosa)* to name just a few. Approaching history not as a mere chronology of facts, he endeavored to capture the context of peoples lives, including their environment and feelings, in an effort to more fully understand history. This method was original and effective. It helped him earn fame but later, when Japan annexed Korea in 1910, it made him a target for repression. Within a few years he was forced into exile in China.

In Shanghai, he continued his studies of history and the

struggle for Korean independence. After the 1 March, 1919 independence movement, Tanjae joined the other exiled nationalists in China and worked for two years advising and helping to found their representative newspaper, *The Independence News*. He soon became discouraged with some of the policies of the government in exile and moved to Peking to study further. While in Peking, researching *A History of Ancient Korea*, he derived an income from writing articles for local newspapers. He met other Korean scholars and historians while in China and is remembered as one who had a great enthusiasm for history. His earnings were meager and resulted in a somewhat less than simple life. Later, in 1922, he lived as a Buddhist monk and studied Buddhist philosophy. Incredibly, within a few years he reportedly became an acknowledged authority in this area. Also, while at the temple, he continued to pursue his studies of Korean history and wrote some additional articles on various related subjects. Over the years, Tanjae became increasingly anti-Japanese as the Japanese continued their pressure during colonization. He wrote, in 1923, a document known as "The Korean Revolutionary Declaration." This letter demanded Koreans' act to restore independence by force to include assassinating Japanese leaders and attacking Japanese establishments. He was later arrested in 1928, and sentenced to ten years in prison for his activities. He spent eight years in a prison, in Lushin China, where he became seriously ill and died in 1936. Tanjae was reportedly buried in his hometown even though his hatred for the Japanese was so strong that he had asked to be cremated, and his ashes scattered at sea, so even in death, he would prevent the Japanese from treading on him.

Tanjae's works have been collected and reprinted since his death. Some say he is even more famous in death than he was in life. It is certain that his efforts were significant and if he were alive, he would be happy to know, his writings continue to inspire and enlighten people, even today, to the importance of Korea's past.

47
Dedicated Journalist

So Chae-p'il
(Dr. Philip Jaisohn, 1866 -1951)

The most celebrated journalist of modern Korea, Dr. Jaisohn was a character of even deeper substance. A renowned independence figure, medical doctor, and later statesman, Dr. Jaisohn effected a significant impact on the political face of Korea in both the nineteenth and twentieth centuries. Beginning with his part in a coup attempt during the Yi Dynasty reign of King Kojong, through the independence movement of 1919 and the post-war government of the new republic, Dr. Jaisohn contributed to positive political change in Korea over a span of seven decades.

An individual of noble birth, Dr. Jaisohn was the second son of So Kwang-on who was once a high official in his county in South Cholla Province. Dr. Jaisohn was born there in Posong county on 28 October, 1866. Early in his childhood, at the age of seven, he moved to Seoul to study the Chinese classics under expert tutelage. Later he moved to Tokyo to study at the Rikugun Toyama Gakko, a Japanese Army School where he enrolled in their junior officers course. During his time there he had frequent contact with Kim Ok-kyun (see chapter 45) who later lead the famous Kapshin

TOP LEFT **Photo of So Chae-p'il, founder of the Independence Club** TOP RIGHT **Periodical of the Independence Club** ABOVE **Korea's first modern newspaper, published both in Korean and in English by So Chae-p'il in the late 19th century**

Coup of 1884. Dr. Jaisohn graduated from the school on 31 May, 1884 and returned to Seoul with a position in the military training bureau. He was soon replaced, however, due to some political maneuvers that worked to his disadvantage.

Within a few months, Dr. Jaisohn became involved in the planning of a coup to break the dominant Chinese influence of Korea and institute major reforms similar to those that contributed to the modernization of Japan. The coup had some Japanese support and the coup members were confident they could succeed. The coup began as planned on 4 December, participants were able to gain control of the king and hold him under guard. They were also able to kill some of the opposition figures. The following day they established a reform government and began instituting the political, social, and economic changes they had waited so long to originate. Their success did not last however, as Chinese forces countered and regained custody of the king after only three days. The coup failed and its leaders were killed or forced to flee. Dr. Jaisohn's role was initially military, he commanded over one hundred troops that held the king under guard until Chinese troops, with far superior numbers, were able to regain control. He also participated in the short lived administration. As a result he too fled to Japan to avoid persecution.

After a short stay in Japan, he traveled to the U.S. to study in April-May of the following year. His life there was itself an incredible story. Reportedly, he first took a job delivering handbills in San Francisco. He met a man who helped him enter a boys' school and prepare for college. By some additional kindness from a professor at Lafayette College, Dr. Jaisohn was able to attend school there and receive room and board in exchange for performing odd jobs. When the professor became ill, Dr. Jaisohn was forced to abandon his studies and look for a new way to earn a living. After a short stay in Philadelphia, he went to Washington D.C. actually intending to see President Cleveland and request his assistance. Strangely enough, while he did not see the president, the president's secretary gave him a letter of introduction that ultimately landed him a position translating Japanese at the Army Medical Library at a good salary. This also provided him the opportunity to study medicine at George Washington University at night. He graduated in 1895 and was the first Korean to receive a medical degree from a U.S. university. Soon afterward, he received an appointment at a local hospital where he was an assistant to the famous Dr. Walter Reed. Dr. Jaisohn also married and became a U.S. citizen during this period.

In the same year, the Japanese won their war with China and increased their influence over Korea. Dr. Jaisohn could now return home without fear of retribution for his part in the 1884 coup. A tremendous welcome awaited him when he arrived in 1896. He was offered important government positions but because of his American citizenship he decided to accept an important advisory role to the government. More importantly, at only thirty years old, he founded the first modern newspaper of Korea, *The Independent*, on 7 April, 1896. The paper was printed in English and Korean and at first, was published three times a week. It was designed to educate the common people and eschewed the use of Chinese characters which were not well-known by the masses and were a symbol of the elitism of the upper class.

In the same year, the Independence Club was established to educate the public, encourage modernization and induce reform in government. Dr. Jaisohn was instrumental in the formation of the club and continued to provide guidance and advice. Unfortunately, Dr. Jaisohn was forced to leave Korea in 1898, because of significant opposition from government officials who were not ready for such reforms.

From America, he continued his independence efforts throughout the Japanese colonial period. At the end of World War II he returned again as a respected leader of Korea and advisor to the government. He continued his efforts until his death in the U.S. in 1951.

Today many personal possessions, photos and writings of Dr. Jaisohn are preserved in the Independence Hall in Ch'onan. There is also a large statue of him next to the

Independence Gate, which he helped construct, in Sodaemun on the west side of Seoul.

His lifelong contributions to the political development and overall advancement of Korea were significant. He shares a distinguished place in Korean history among those who spared no sacrifice to achieve independence and lift Korea into the modern world.

48
Indefatigable Independence Fighter

Yi Sang-jae
(Wolnam, 1850 -1927)

Diplomat, independence fighter, and politician, this dedicated citizen spent over forty years in the service of his country inspiring others towards patriotism and independence. He played a key political role in developing policies at the turn of the century and was active in both the Independence Club and the 1919 Independence Movement during the Japanese colonial period.

Born in South Ch'ungch'ong Province, in Hansan-myon, Soch'on-gun, Wolnam grew up in a traditional Confucian environment. His life spanned a period of particular change in Korean political and economic development. He spent most of his teenage years living during the reign of the Taewongun, experiencing the Christian persecutions, the corruption of the Confucian government and the xenophobia of the Hermit Kingdom. In his twenties, he witnessed the opening of Korea to foreigners and the benefits and dilemmas of modernization. By his early thirties, he was eager to observe the progress of more modern countries and help Korea take advantage of such knowledge to assist in its own development. In 1881, he traveled to Japan as part of a group

Photo of Yi Sang-jae, patriot and organizing member of the Independence Club

assembled to observe such things in that country. He absorbed much about Western technology and was able to help implement an adaptation of it in Korea, some three years later, when Korea's first Postmaster General awarded him a position as the chief of a new communications station in the port city of Inch'on. Within three years, he was quickly promoted to a position as a senior secretary at the country's first embassy in America.

Wolnam returned with a better understanding of modern society and Western technology and was interested in spreading these ideas in Korea. He became friends with other Christian men of similar philosophy and intent, some very famous in their own right, among them were So Chae-p'il and Rhee Syng-man. When So Chae-p'il founded the Independence Club in 1896, to educate the public, encourage modernization and influence reform in government, Wolnam was very active and became a key leader of the club.

The club got off to a great start quickly raising funds to build an Independence Gate and Independence Hall on the site where Korea used to welcome visiting delegations from China. Their efforts were successful and the cornerstone was laid in November of that year. The gate was completed and still stands as an important monument. It has been expanded with an attached park in western Seoul. As the club became more popular and membership swelled, the government became more concerned for its very existence. The club's positions on free speech, neutral foreign policy, cessation of foreign interference in Korean internal matters and others, caused problems for the existing government. The government soon ordered the club disbanded and Wolnam and many other leaders of the organization were arrested and imprisoned. Mass demonstrations were organized to effect their release but this only provided the excuse for the government to use more force to suppress them.

Wolnam turned to political activities via a different platform. With the help of others, like Rhee Syng-man and some American missionaries, they established the YMCA in Seoul, in 1903, which among other things, encouraged nationalism and patriotism among Christian young men. The group sponsored political as well as social programs and inspired other spin-off groups with similar goals.

Leading up to and following the March 1919, independence movement Wolnam continued his efforts. Although the Japanese had frustrated the independence movement itself, Wolnam did not give up the struggle. The year 1920 saw a dramatic growth in Korean newspapers. Where there had been only one paper authorized by the Japanese government for the ten years beginning in 1910, three new Korean language newspapers appeared in 1920; the *Chosun Ilbo*, the *Dong-A Ilbo*, and the *Shisa Shinmun*. By 1924, Wolnam was part of a group that took over management of the *Chosun Ilbo* and used it to speak out against Japanese colonial policy. This prompted much pressure from the Japanese who used censorship, and other forms of pressure against the paper before finally closing it in 1940 some years after Wolnam's death.

Committed to education as the method to a strong, prosperous, and independent Korea, in 1922, Wolnam, Yi Sunghun, and others started a foundation to raise funds for a private university in Korea. Again however, their efforts had been spoiled by harsh Japanese reaction and rules making such efforts difficult if not impossible to accomplish. Some years later though, American missionaries were able to establish facilities such as Ewha and Sookmyung Women's colleges.

Today a larger than life-size statue of him stands in downtown Seoul at Citizens Park in front of the Royal Shrine (Chongmyo) on Chong-no Street. He did his part to help educate Koreans about the world around them and fought relentlessly to keep his country from being overcome by it.

49
Korea's Joan of Arc

Yu Kwan-sun
(1904-1920)

One of Korea's most famous women independence fighters, Yu's contributions were significant for a woman so young. It's difficult to imagine how one person could have done so much at such an early age. Her ability to organize and incite people to action resulted in key resistance to Japanese colonialism during the 1 March, 1919 Independence Movement. Unfortunately for her however, those efforts cost her freedom when Japanese police arrested her and, after many days of torture, she ultimately died in prison. Her sacrifices are celebrated throughout the country and she is well remembered as a dedicated woman who accomplished much for Korean independence in her short life. Her unflinching resolve, even in the face of death, has often earned her the title of Korean Joan of Arc.

The little village near Ch'onan, in South Ch'ungch'ong Province, was her birthplace on 26 March. It was a humble home in a small farming village tucked away behind some hills in the countryside. She was the second of four children and the only daughter in her family. Her father, Yu Chung-kwon, was a respectable citizen and civic leader of the small

ABOVE Yu Kwan-sun and her classmates at Ehwa Girls' School (Top row far right)   LEFT Yu in Sodaemun Prison in Seoul just before she died in 1920

community.

In March of 1916, her father decided to take advantage of a chance to send his daughter to school in Seoul. Yu was admitted to Ewha Girls' School in Chong-dong, Seoul, in April of that year. She did very well in her studies and she used her first few summer vacations to return home and teach local villagers to read and expose many of them to Western science and geography which was quite different from their traditional Chinese classical education.

The following year, 1919, the fervor for independence was reaching a climax in Korea. On 22 January, King Kojong, who had abdicated his throne in 1907, died in Seoul amidst rumors he had been poisoned by the Japanese. Many people truly mourned the death including Yu and her classmates. The underground independence movement benefitted from the incident and, capitalizing on the momentum, decided to stage mass demonstrations and declare independence from Japan on 1 March, just two days before the scheduled funeral of the king. They drafted a declaration and distributed copies around Korea and to independence groups in Tokyo and Shanghai. Yu and her friends pledged to participate in the movement and on 1 March were part of the mass demonstrations at Pagoda Park in downtown Seoul, declaring independence from Japan. Many people, including some of the teachers and many of the students from Yu's school were arrested that day and the school was forced to close. Determined not to give up, she returned to her hometown and resolved to continue the movement in the countryside.

Although she initially met with resistance because of her youth and the fact that local police were watching carefully, she eventually won support of the local people. With the help of local church group elders she planned and organized a mass demonstration similar to the one in Seoul, this one scheduled for 1 March by the lunar calendar which happened to fall on 1 April. Traveling from village to village she informed people from Ch'ongju to Chinch'on of the planned demonstration and informed the people to send representatives to her village for additional planning. She announced the signal would be a torch relayed from the mountain tops. The night before the scheduled demonstrations she personally climbed the mountain and ignited the fire that signaled the meetings the following day at the Aunae market. She addressed the crowd, read the declaration and led a march through town. The Japanese responded with force killing many people, including Yu's parents, and arresting many others including Yu.

She was first sent to Ch'onan prison where she was tortured for many days before transfer to Kongju prison. She was later tried and sentenced to three years in prison which she spent in Sodaemun prison in Seoul. Prison life was too much for her though, and she died there on 12 October the next year at the age of sixteen. Her last words were reportedly "Japan shall fall." The Japanese reportedly then tore her limbs from her body into many pieces.

There are quite a few memorials to Yu throughout Korea, the largest and most famous of which is her memorial shrine near Ch'onan. The shrine is beautifully landscaped with a small plaza with a large statue at the base of a mountain with the shrine located just a short walk further up the mountain. In the shrine itself, a large portrait of Yu is on exhibit. To the left of the shrine is a path that winds its way further up the mountain to Yu's gravesite. The path continues for a pleasant walk up the mountain to the very top where a monument marks the spot where Yu gave the famous signal, by torch, that began the independence movement in that area. From that spot there is an incredible view which makes it easy to see how a fire would be visible for miles from that point. From the entrance of the shrine, it is just a short drive or even walk to Yu's birthplace, which has been remodeled and preserved in the fashion it was when she lived there. Not far from this area is the National Independence Hall which has a display of Yu including a mock up of the prison cell she spent time and ultimately died in. In the capital, there is a large statue of her located near Dongguk University in Changch'ung-dong at the north entrance of tunnel #2. Yu is standing, in this statue, in her famous pose, arm outstretched, torch in hand.

This extraordinary young woman with an indefatigable spirit accomplished much, in her short life, to inspire the Korean people and help them endure the hardships of occupation. Her actions gained the admiration of everyday people and helped them to persevere when they needed hope most.

50
Patriotic Martyr
Yun Pong-gil
(1908 –1932)

A simple man with a great love for his country, Yun loved and struggled for a Korea he never really knew. His short life did not provide time for him to achieve greatness in more traditional pursuits. For Yun, caught up in the fervor of independence, fame was a result of his bold act in support of that movement, when in April 1932, he bombed a Japanese delegation visiting China to celebrate the Japanese emperor's birthday. Yun was later executed for his act but he has been celebrated as a great patriot in Korea for providing courage and hope to Koreans everywhere who were fighting relentlessly for independence from Japanese colonial rule.

Yun was born on 21 June (23 May by lunar calendar), in the small village of Yesan-gun, South Ch'ungch'ong Province. He was the first son born to Yun Hwang-kong and Kim Won-jo. His family boasted a proud ancestry dating back to Yun Kwan, a famous military general of the Koryo Dynasty. His family ensured young Yun received the traditional classic education. At age five he attended a local school *(sodang)* where he studied the Chinese classics from a local teacher, Yun Hyong, who happened to be his uncle. The

236 / KOREANS TO REMEMBER

Portrait of Yun Pong-gil, who were fighting relentlessly for independence from Japanese colonial rule

Taken captive after his bombing attack on Japanese officials in 1932

following year his mother assumed control of his education and taught him Chinese characters from the "Thousand Character Text," a primer for such study. By 1918 he was ready for elementary school and attended the Toksan Common School nearby. However, in 1919, after the initiation of the independence movement, his parents made him resign from school in protest to the Japanese education policy of that period. For the next few years he engaged in a combination of self-study and personal instruction in the Confucian classics from Ch'oe Pyong-t'ae. In 1921 he returned to more formal school at Och'i lecture hall in Toksan and studied more Chinese classics under instruction from Song Chu-rok. In this way the personality and philosophy of Yun was formed. From that time forward he planned to devote his time to composing Chinese poetry and applying his knowledge to life works.

In the spring of 1922, at the early age of fourteen, he married a local girl, Pae Yong-sun. Later that year in July, some of Yun's hardwork began to pay off when he won local literary recognition for his entry at an exhibition of Chinese poems at the Och'i lecture hall in Toksan. In 1925, he became a teacher at the Och'i school and it was there that he solidified his nationalist feelings and deep patriotic philosophy by studying biographies of famous Korean government officials. He took on the task of educating others, especially farmers, to help Korea advance as a nation and with the hope of someday regaining Korea's independence.

Yun worked hard for the farmers, eventually establishing Wolchinhoe, a monthly working group to help educate and organize farmers to improve their standard of living. The concept of Wolchinhoe was the forerunner of the modern Saemaul Movement instituted by President Park Chung-hee almost forty years later. Yun later wrote a three volume textbook for farmers and in February 1928, not yet twenty years of age, he established a headquarters for rejuvenating the agricultural community. It was at this time he started keeping a diary which provided many details of the last few years of his life. In April of 1929, he became the president of

Wolchinhoe and continued to help educate farmers and spread nationalism through his movement. As a result he came under closer scrutiny of the Japanese police who applied much pressure for Yun to stop such activity. As the pressure increased Yun decided to move to Shanghai China and contact independence fighters there. He left on 6 March, 1930, and wrote the following sentence in his diary before departing: "It is impossible for a full grown man who became a Buddhist monk to return home alive." It appears Yun had already decided his fate and left for Shanghai looking for a method to express his devotion to the independence movement.

Koreans in China helped Yun find a job at a factory with many Korean employees. Yun quickly organized them into a committee to help expand the labor movement. He met with nationalist leaders such as Kim Koo and planned ways to spread nationalism and Japanese resistance. Yun joined the Independence Party, and in 1932, took a job as a grocer to closely surveille local Japanese troops. On 26 April of that year, the Shanghai daily newspaper published an announcement of a birthday celebration in Hongkou Park in Shanghai, in honor of the Japanese emperor. Within a few days Korean independence leaders were plotting resistance action to coincide with the celebration. Yun scouted the area and developed a plan to carry out a bombing of the ceremony. The plan was approved and on 28 April he ate his last breakfast with Kim Koo and other leaders, prepared the necessary materials, and departed for the park. He arrived there without problem and took a position near the grandstand. At 11:40, just after the Japanese national anthem, Yun threw a bomb at the grandstand killing the commander of Japanese troops in Shanghai and the head of the Japanese Residents Association. Many others were injured including the commander of the Third Fleet of the Japanese Navy and the diplomatic minister in Shanghai. Yun was quickly arrested and later taken to Osaka on 21 June. He was sentenced to death and executed within the year on 19 December and his body was reportedly thrown in a dump.

Yun's act stirred the Korean spirit for independence and is highly regarded among Koreans. There are many shrines to him in Korea today, the most noteworthy are the main memorial and museum built for him in Yangjae-dong in southern Seoul. Further south, at the Independence Hall in Ch'onan, there are detailed displays relating to him and the bombing incident. Also at his hometown in Toksan, his birthplace has been refurbished and a large memorial with adjoining museum is open to the public. In 1992, the Korean government issued a commemorative stamp which coincided with the sixtieth anniversary of the bombing incident.

Index

Ahn Kyon, 194
Ahn Tu-hui, 212
Cairo Declaration, 211
Chajang, 56
Chikchisa Temple, 121, 124
Chip'yonjon, 51
Ch'oe Kyu-ha, 8, 10
Ch'oe Shi-hyong, 148
Ch'oe Shin-ji, 151
Choltusan Shrine, 118, 120, 164, 208
Ch'omsongdae, 55
Ch'ondogyo, 172, 197
Chong Yo-rip, 123
Chosun Ilbo, 189, 198, 229
Christian persecutions, 37, 119, 163, 226
Chu Hsi, 158
Ch'usach'e, 166, 168
Civil Rule Party, 42
Daehan Maeil Shinmun, 219
Daewoo, 134-137
Democratic Justice Party, 19, 32
Democratic Liberal Party, 19
Democratic Party, 41
Dong-A Ilbo, 155, 187, 189, 190, 198, 229
Ewha Womans University, 185, 234
Francesca Donner, 26, 28
Guomindang, 155
Haeinsa Temple, 124
Hallim haksa, 151
Ham Sok-hon, 24, 28, 69
Han-gul, 49, 52
Hideyoshi Invasion, 94

Hungsadan, 185, 203
Hunmin jongum, 50
Hwangsong Shinmun, 219
Hwarang, 81
Hyonch'ungsa Shrine, 95
Hyundai, 129-132
Ihwajang, 28
Imo Kullan Incident, 143
Independence Club, 27, 203, 219, 222, 224, 226, 227, 228
Independence Gate, 225, 228
Independence Hall, 204, 208, 212, 224
Independence News, The, 220
Independent, The, 222, 224
Itō Hirobumi, 205, 207
Jurchens, 78
Kapshin Coup, 47, 216, 221, 223
Khitans, 76, 77
Kim Chae-kyu, 10, 24
Kim Il-sung, 212
Kim Ki-su, 141
Kim Kyu-shik, 212
Kim Sang-man, 189
Kim Shin, 210
King Ch'olchong, 34, 45, 153
King Chongjo, 163
King Chongjong, 49
King Chungjong, 191
King Honjong, 168
King Hyonjong, 77
King Injo, 45
King Kongmin, 65, 71, 158
King Mokchong, 76

King Munmu, 81
King Shinmun, 102
King Shinu, 65, 72, 158
King Sonjo, 124
King Sunjong, 48
King T'aejong, 49, 51
King Uija, 85
King Yonsan, 191
Korea Broadcasting System, 185, 186
Korea Democratic Party, 190
Korea University, 187, 188, 189
Korean Independence Party, 211
Korean Military Academy, 7
Korean national anthem, 177, 178, 180
Korean People's Party, 211
Korean War, 5, 31
Koryo ch'ongja, 59
Kungye, 60
Kwanch'ang, 86
Kwangbok (Liberation) Army, 211
Kwangju Incident, 10, 15
Kyongbok Palace, 45, 53, 63
Kyongbuk High School, 29
Kyonhwon, 60
Later Koguryo, 60, 151
Later Paekche, 60, 151
Later Three Kingdoms, 151
Liberal Party, 41
March First Movement, 220, 226, 230
Naksongdae, 75
National Party, 42
New Democratic Party, 14, 18, 42
New Korea Democratic Party, 19
New Peoples Party, 42
Ojuk'on, 108, 194
Orini, 173
Paejae School, 27
Popular Party, 42
Posong College, 172, 189
Provisional government, 27, 209
Pueblo, 24
Queen Chindok, 57
Queen Chinsong, 151
Queen Min, 37, 45, 48, 211

Rangoon Incident, 10
Red Turbans, 64
Reunification Democratic Party, 19
Richard Strauss, 180
Russo-Japanese War, 48, 203, 207
Saektonghoe, 173
Saemaul Movement, 237
Samguk Yusa, 55
Shijo, 153
Shinminhoe, 211
Shin Ton, 71, 72
Shirhak (Practical Learning), 161, 163, 215
Shisa Shinmun, 229
Sino-Japanese War, 48, 197, 201, 204, 216
Sodang, 235
Sol Ch'ong, 102
Songgyungwan, 103, 149, 156, 163, 219
Sonjukkyo Bridge, 157, 159
Son Pyong-hui, 172
Taesong School, 203
Tonghak, 115, 145-148, 172, 195, 197, 209, 211
Tonghak Rebellion, 172, 211
Tongjesa, 153, 155
Tosan Sowon, 104, 105, 106
Toyotomi Hideyoshi, 123
Treaty of Kanghwa, 47
Treaty of Portsmouth, 207
Turtle Ship, 92-95
Uisang, 101
Unification National Party, 132
Vietnam War, 23
Weng Fang-gang, 167
Wolchinhoe, 238
Yang Ti, 89
Yi Ki-bung, 5
Yi Saek, 156
Yi Shi-yong, 190
YMCA, 185, 228
Yonsei University, 157
Yuk Yong-soo, 22, 24
Yun Kwan, 235
Yushin Constitution, 14, 24

The Fifty Figures in Chronological Order

560-620	Ulchi Mundok	1855-1935	Chi Sok-yong
595-673	Kim Yu-shin	1866-1951	So Chae-p'il
600-660	Kyebaek	1875-1965	Rhee Syng-man
610-647	Queen Sondok	1876-1949	Kim Koo
617-686	Wonhyo	1878-1939	Ahn Ch'ang-ho
857-?	Ch'oe Ch'i-won	1879-1910	Ahn Chung-gun
877-943	Wang Kon	1879-1944	Han Yong-un
948-1031	Kang Kam-ch'an	1880-1936	Shin Ch'ae-ho
1316-1389	Ch'oe Yong	1891-1955	Kim Song-su
1335-1408	Yi Song-gye	1892-1950	Yi Kwang-su
1337-1392	Chong Mong-ju	1892-?	Chong In-bo
1397-1450	King Sejong	1897-1941	Hong Nanp'a
1501-1570	Yi Hwang	1897-1990	Yun Po-son
1504-1551	Shin Saimdang	1899-1931	Pang Chong-hwan
1536-1584	Yi Yi	1899-1966	Chang Myon
1544-1610	Samyongdang	1904-1920	Yu Kwan-sun
1545-1598	Yi Sun-shin	1906-1965	Ahn Eak-tay
1762-1836	Chong Yak-yong	1908-1932	Yun Pong-gil
1786-1856	Kim Chong-hui	1915-	Chung Ju-yung
1820-1898	Yi Ha-ung	1917-1979	Park Chung-hee
1821-1846	Kim Tae-gon	1924-	Kim Dae-jung
1824-1864	Ch'oe Che-u	1927-	Kim Young-sam
1850-1927	Yi Sang-jae	1931-	Chun Doo-hwan
1851-1894	Kim Ok-kyun	1932-	Roh Tae-woo
1852-1919	King Kojong	1936-	*Kim Woo-choong*

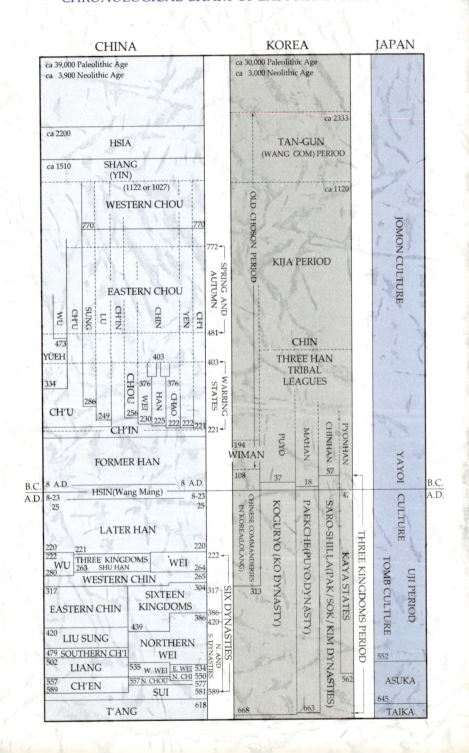

CHRONOLOGICAL CHART OF EAST ASIAN HISTORY II

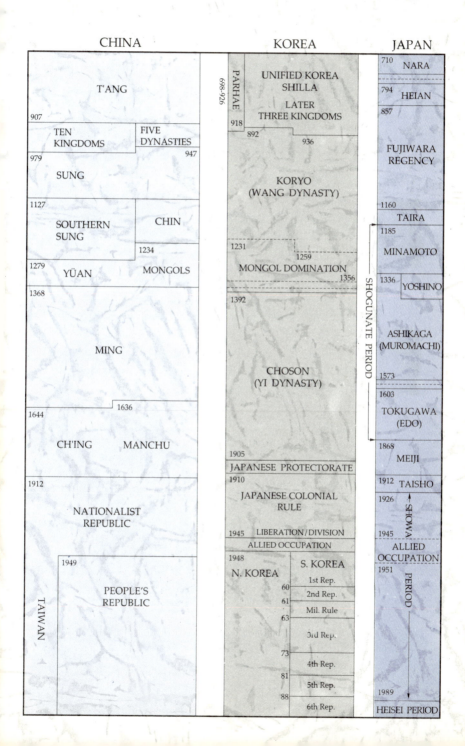